BACKCOUNTRY BIKING
in the Canadian Rockies

Text by Gerhardt Lepp
Maps by Jo-Ann Draper
Drawings by Colynn Kerr

ROCKY MOUNTAIN BOOKS - CALGARY

A WORD OF THANKS

We wish to extend our thanks to everyone who had encouraging words for our project. The book would never have been written without that support.

A very special thanks to our friend Jeff Grutz who shared many trails and hours of discussing this book, as well as his knowledge of the Eastern Slopes.

Many people from Kananaskis Country and the National Parks reviewed the manuscript to ensure accuracy. Ron Chamney, Eric Kuhn, Dave Zevick, Scott Mair, Rod Jaeger and others from the ranger and visitor services staff in Kananaskis Country were most helpful.

Many thanks to Martha McCallum at Parks Canada who distributed the manuscript to the individual parks for their perusal. Thanks to Bill Vroom, Lynn Yeates, Brian Hall, Michael Morris, Tom Davidson, Don Sears, Perry Davis, Steve Kun, Doug Wellock and others at Parks Canada for their helpful remarks.

Morris Lemire and Peter Allen were very helpful in reviewing the manuscript and helping me with the editing.

Thanks to Alex Berenyi who wrote the section, "The Alloy Horse - What Kind of Bike Do I Need?" for his special knowledge of mountain bikes and their maintenance.

Gillean Daffern, the publisher, provided knowledge of the trails. Mike Sawyer provided information about trail impact and on the politics of mountain biking.

Thanks to all our friends and fellow ski patrollers and LIABCS (Life In A Beer Commercial Society), who shared the many trails we lead them down. Thanks to Gord and Deb Ritchie who endured the thirteen hour epic over Evan-Thomas pass - we were ninety percent sure there was a trail there.

Thanks to Bev and Rob McKenzie who waited for us at the trailhead of the Skoki Valley trail as we cycled through the rain and snow and provided warmth, tea and cookies for two cold and stiff cyclists. Thanks to you all.

Published by Rocky Mountain Books, 106 Wimbledon Crescent, Calgary, Alberta
Printed and bound in Canada by Hignell Printing Limited, Winnipeg

ISBN 0-9690038-8-9

CONTENTS

PREFACE

It all started in Hawaii. Jo-Ann and I had gone there, along with ten thousand other people to run the Honolulu Marathon. The day before the race various merchants displayed their wares in Kapiolani Park and before we knew it we were both taking a mountain bike out for a test drive through the park. I had never ridden one before but after less than two minutes in the saddle I was grinning from ear to ear.

Obviously thousands of other people felt the same way. Mountain bikes now account for over half of the total bicycle sales in western Canada. Actually I should qualify that - there is a difference between a "bike you can ride in the mountains" and a "wide handlebar bike" built to ride the wave of a new fashion. I say that because I don't want to feel responsible if a fit of enthusiasm overcomes you and you ride some hundred and fifty dollar department store special up the Elbow River and get stranded a long way from your car when it self destructs.

Like everyone else, we wondered where to ride our new toys. Anyone who says that you can ride a mountain bike anywhere probably hasn't ridden in the Canadian Rocky Mountains very much. Most of the steep hiking trails along the Continental Divide are not suitable for a bicycle. However, we discovered that mountain bikes offer a new way to discover the foothills, the valley bottom roads, the grassy ridges and the more gentle parts of the Canadian Rockies. I hope your own backcountry biking experiences in the Rockies make you smile from ear to ear.

JASPER NATIONAL PARK

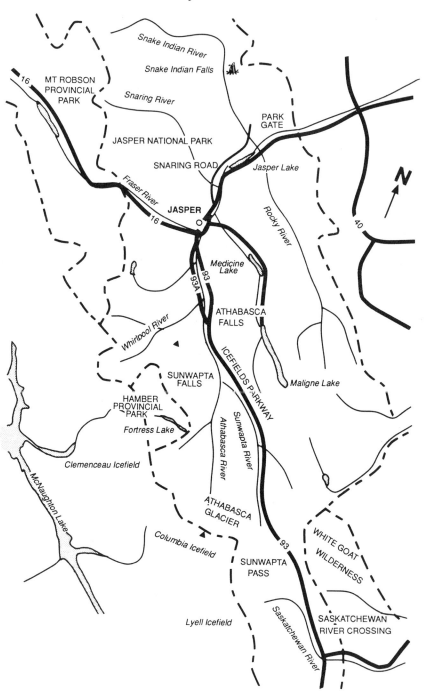

YOHO, KOOTENAY & BANFF
NATIONAL PARKS

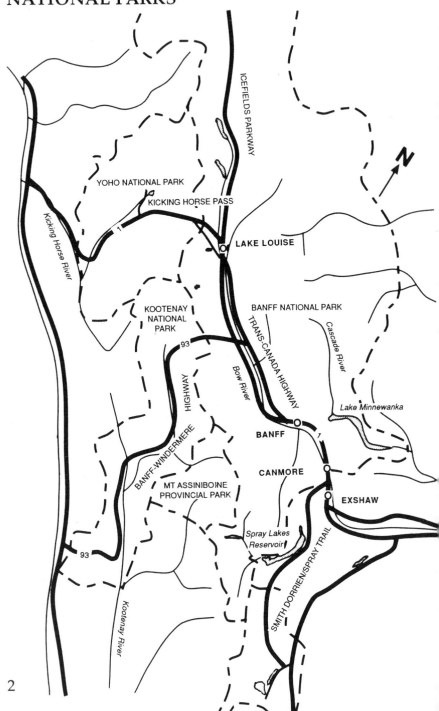

KANANASKIS COUNTRY

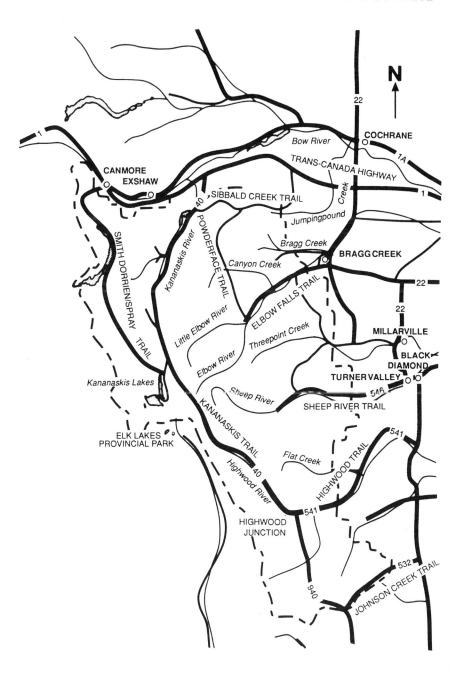

N

COCHRANE

22

1A

Bow River

TRANS-CANADA HIGHWAY

1

CANMORE
EXSHAW

SIBBALD CREEK TRAIL

Jumpingpound

40

Creek

Bragg Creek

BRAGG CREEK

POWDERFACE TRAIL

Kananaskis River

Canyon Creek

22

22

SMITH DORRIEN/SPRAY

TRAIL

Little Elbow River

ELBOW FALLS TRAIL

Threepoint Creek

MILLARVILLE

Elbow River

BLACK
DIAMOND

Kananaskis Lakes

Sheep River

TURNER VALLEY

546

SHEEP RIVER TRAIL

KANANASKIS TRAIL

ELK LAKES
PROVINCIAL PARK

541

Flat Creek

HIGHWOOD TRAIL

40

Highwood River

541

HIGHWOOD
JUNCTION

532

940

JOHNSON CREEK TRAIL

OLDMAN, CROWSNEST-CASTLE
& WATERTON NATIONAL PARK

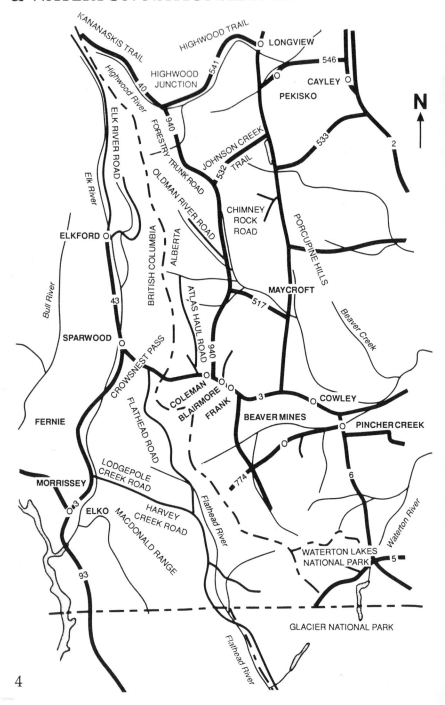

EQUIPMENT & MAINTENANCE

THE ALLOY HORSE by Alex Berenyi
WHAT KIND OF A BIKE DO I NEED ?

Call them what you will: cruisers, clunkers, mountain bikes, trail bicycles or ballooners. What all off-road bikes have in common are fat tires. That alone makes them more suitable for rough terrain, because such tires absorb shock and are more stable on wet or loose surfaces. Most other changes in the evolution of mountain bikes have been refinements to existing racing or touring bicycle technology as the form came to more closely follow the function.

As tough as they are, there is nothing on a mountain bike that cannot be worn out or broken with rough and repeated use. You'll enjoy off road cycling more and spend less time and money on maintenance if you buy a quality machine.

The most important decision in selecting a bike is the choice of frame size. Frames are measured from the centre of the crank axle to the top of the seat tube (the frame tube running from the crank up to the seat, but not including the adjustable seatpost). They vary in size from 16 or 17 inches (46 or 48 cm) to 21 or 23 inches (56 or 58 cm). Any good bike will be available in a selection of at least three or four sizes. Stand with your legs straddling the top tube of the bike. With your feet flat on the ground in normal shoes, you should have at least 2 inches of clearance between your crotch and the top tube. For extreme riding, we recommend up to 4 inches of clearance, both for safety and for the improved responsiveness of a smaller frame. Either way, your mountain bike will be smaller than your road bike. If it isn't, it's going to hurt.

FRAME & FORKS

The most important requirement in the design of an off-road bicycle is durability, yet it should not weigh much more than 14 kilograms. The most important elements of that design are the frame and forks. They must be very strong to withstand the shock of rough terrain, unexpected obstacles and fast, rough downhill descents. In order to increase rigidity, most of the tubes on all-terrain bikes are of larger diameter than those on road bikes

The majority of off-road bikes are built of either high tensile steel, manganese alloy steel or chrome molybdenum alloy steel, in order of increasing strength. Cro-moly is significantly stronger, allowing reduced wall thickness in the tubing. The frame is thus lighter and stronger. Low and medium priced bikes (under $700) are commonly made with some combination of high tensile mangalloy or cro-moly tubes in different parts of the frame. The greater your weight or the rougher your riding, the more need you have of a stronger frame.

A new generation of off-road bicycles are being made with aircraft grade aluminum alloy tubing in the frame, instead of steel. These bikes can be identified by the extra large diameter of their tubing, which provides greater stiffness than steel frames, equal strength, and reduced weight.

The type of material in the tubing is identified on most good frames by a sticker near the top of the seat tube. While there are both welded and brazed mountain bike frames, there is no practical difference between the two building techniques.

Traditionally the best mountain bikes have been either hand built or Japanese made, and all have had Japanese components. Less favorable foreign exchange rates have started a shift of lower and midpriced production to Taiwan to reduce costs. Taiwan quality control in frame building varies from high quality comparable to Japanese to very low quality. Taiwan component quality is not good enough yet to be considered acceptable for serious use. However, expect that to change as their technology continues to improve.

The design of the frame and forks will vary depending on the manufacturer and the intended use. In general, a bike built for maximum stability on fast, rough descents will have a longer wheelbase and chainstays, and a shallower head tube angle (the forks will angle out to the front more). Such a bike must sacrifice a certain amount of responsiveness to gain its stability. A bike designed for greater low-speed maneuverability and responsiveness will have a shorter wheelbase and chainstays and a steeper head tube angle. This will also position the rider's weight better for very steep climbing. The majority of off-road bikes available today are designed to provide a useful compromise between the two extremes.

WHEELS

Strength and light weight in the wheels is even more important than in the frame. Fat, shock absorbing tires provide much of the required durability. Dirt riding requires the wider 26 x 1.90 to 26 x 2.215 tires with an aggressive, full knobby tread. For street riding or mixed use a narrower 26 x 1.75 or 26 x 1.5 tire with smooth centre tread may be preferred for lighter weight and reduced rolling resistance. Heavier 14 gauge spokes are standard equipment, and must be kept properly tightened.

All good mountain bike rims are made of aluminum alloy which saves as much as one kilogram per wheel over steel. Cheaper bikes with steel rims are not suitable for off-road riding because they bend too easily and are too heavy for safe bike handling. If you rent a bike as an introduction to the sport be sure to get one with alloy rims. The brake pads also grab far better on aluminum.

The hubs on all but the cheapest bikes will also be aluminum. Most mountain bike hubs have solid axles (preferably cro-moly) secured by regular nuts, rather than the lighter quick release type. The greater strength of the solid axle is particularly important in the rear hub. Quick release front wheels are becoming more common, making storage and transportation easier. Many of the mid to high priced mountain bikes have sealed hub bearings. They are either the standard ball bearing and cone type protected by a labyrinth seal, or O-ring seal or the cassette bearing type which is generally of higher precision and can be replaced as a complete unit. They are often described by the terms "sealed mechanism bearing" for the former and "sealed bearing" for the latter. As this terminology makes the difference between the two about as clear as the mud you ride through, we prefer the terms "O-ring sealed bearing" and "cassette sealed bearing", respectively.

Sealed bearings require less maintenance, especially in the wet and dirty conditions so often encountered by mountain bikers. However, they are not maintenance free. If you anticipate riding in wet or dirty conditions at any time, it is strongly recommended that you pre-service your bearings for maximum water resistance. This applies to old as well as brand-new bikes. The factory supplied grease is usually neither heavy enough, nor is there enough of it to really stand up to dirty use. Use a heavy, sticky grease designed to be as water resistant as possible.

O-ring sealed bearings are all serviced with the same tools and techniques as standard bearings. Most cassette sealed bearings use the same tools, although a few have special purpose adjusting tools made for them which are optional (for convenience) rather than essential. All of the good cassette bearings can be cleaned and regreased without being removed from the hub. The axle and outer dust cover are first removed. The seal can then be popped out with a pin or the tip of a very sharp knife blade. The bearing can then be cleaned with solvent or a spray lubricant such as WD-40. It should then be dried and generously repacked with good grease. The seal is snapped back into place with finger pressure, and the axle and outer dust seals (if your hub has them) reassembled.

BRAKES

Mountain bikes require greater stopping power than road bikes. Most are equipped with cantilever brakes, a type of high leverage centre pull brake which pivot on a post brazed directly onto the frame and forks. They are very close to the contact point on the rim for reduced flex. The brake cables are heavy gauge to reduce stretch. The brake levers on the handlebars may be either motorcycle levers such as Tomaselli and Magura, or a similar strong design. Such a brake system gives a feeling akin to power brakes.

Some bikes are equipped with roller-cam brakes, a variation on the cantilever which is actuated by a V-shaped cam instead of a cross cable. These brakes have greater power than cantilevers, and they don't stick out to the side where lurking rocks and trees could break them off. On the other hand, they are more difficult to adjust and more sensitive to jamming by debris thrown up from the trail - besides, how much braking power can you really use before you lose control on loose dirt, especially on the front wheel? Small nylon covers are available to protect the cam, and these tend to eliminate the jamming. A new variation on the roller-cam brake is the U-brake - essentially a heavy-duty centre-pull brake which fits on the same mounts as a roller-cam. Although too early to tell at the time of this writing, this brake may combine the advantages of the other two without the disadvantages.

GEARING

One of the most important considerations in setting up a mountain bike is the selection of gear range. Very low gears are required for steep terrain or low speed maneuvering on uneven ground. For this reason mountain bikes are usually equipped with a triple front crank to provide 15 or 18 gears. Good quality cranks will be cotterless aluminum with replaceable chainrings.

The smallest inner chainring, which provides your low gear, must be 28 teeth or smaller. A typical stock combination is 26/36/46 teeth compared with 42/52 on the average road bike. You may prefer even lower gearing for rough riding and grinding up really long hills in the mountains. The inner chainring can be changed to as small as 24 teeth.

The freewheel on the rear hub may have either 5 or 6 cogs ranging from a small or high gear of 13 teeth to a large or low gear of 34 teeth, with 14/30 or 14/32 being most common. Once again these are interchangeable, with cogs as large as 38 teeth available, however anything larger than 34 tends to adversely affect shifting performance.

Bio-Pace chain rings, which are a modified oval shape instead of round, are designed to smooth out the natural unevenness of human legs pedalling mechanical cranks. They are possibly more beneficial on road bikes where you are likely to be maintaining an even cadence for extended periods of time. Their only disadvantage is that the small chainring cannot be made any smaller than 28 teeth (26 on the new model, which is rounder). If you have need of lower gearing, a round 24 tooth chainring works fine with two larger Bio-Pace rings.

The crank axle and bearings, or bottom bracket, may be either unsealed or the O-ring sealed type, which are quite effective. The cassette sealed bearing type are expensive and not very common, but certainly the best.

Because the drive train on a mountain bike operates under such dirty conditions, it wears faster than on a road bike even if well maintained. Chains, freewheels and rear derailleurs are particularly vulnerable. The best chains such as Shimano, DID and Sedis are recommended for safety. However the best freewheels will not last much longer than the more common mid-priced ones, under the abusive conditions of dirt riding.

Both front and rear derailleurs must be designed to accommodate the very wide gear range. The front derailleurs have a wider cage which curves down almost to the chain stay to leave room for the chain on the smallest chainring. The rear derailleurs have an extra long arm between the top and bottom rollers to handle the varying amount of chain slack as gears are shifted.

Almost all of the Japanese mountain bike derailleurs currently on the market will work very well. The one new design is the click-stop shift selecting systems which have recently become available for mountain bikes. The shift levers have definite clicks for each gear, so that the rider need not worry about getting the rear derailleur exactly aligned on the cog after a shift. These systems all require very precise installation, adjustment and alignment of frame and components. They are very pleasant to use, but at the time of writing it is too early to predict whether they will stand up to the rigors of off-road abuse.

The gear shift levers are located on the handlebars close to the grips so that they can be moved with the thumbs with both hands still on the bars. This is necessary for stable control.

STEERING

Mountain bike handlebars are all quite wide to provide steering leverage. They point almost straight out, rather than curving back, giving a stable, partly forward leaning riding position. A more upright riding position would be very tiring on longer rides and would not provide enough traction on the front wheel. The welded bullmoose or triangular bar is most common, the adjustable stem and bar construction allowing modification of the riding position. The bars can be cut to any desired length if you find them too wide.

The steering bearings, or head set, are usually the loose bearing type, with the better ones having a labyrinth or O-ring seal.

PEDALS & SADDLE

Possibly the most important components on any bike are the ones in contact with the rider. Pedals on mountain bikes have a wide platform with a serrated cage to reduce slippage. The better ones have O-ring seals on the bearings, and a few even have cassette sealed bearings. Toe clips are recommended for those aggressive riders who want to be faster than a speeding train or able to leap tall hills in a single bound (and who also understand the consequences in an unexpected crash). Toe clips are usually used with a smaller pedal.

Mountain bikes are usually equipped with anatomically padded touring saddles covered with either vinyl or the tougher leather. There are many wider saddles available for those who find these too narrow, but the very soft saddles with springs may be too bouncy for some riders. The wider women's touring seats are an excellent choice. Leather touring saddles such as the Ideale 92 are very comfortable after they are broken in, but they do require treatment with leather conditioner and they should not be exposed to rain too often without a cover. The search for the perfect saddle may be long and painful, but it's worth it.

All mountain bikes have quick release seat post bolts which allow rapid adjustment of the seat height to suit varying terrain. The Hite-Rite seat locator is a spring loaded device which allows you to adjust the seat height with one hand while riding. This handy device is much favored by the Faster-Than-A-Speeding-Train types, as well as anyone who wants to slow down a potential seat-and-seatpost thief.

ACCESSORIES

Accessories increase the usefulness of any bicycle. Water bottles are very important. Mount two or three for longer distance rides. Use the heavy gauge aluminum cages as the light ones will break with rough use. The cageless or velcro mount bottles are also effective.

A rear carrier is required if a load is carried. It is unstable and tiring to carry a heavy weight on your back for long rides. Recommended are carriers with four point mounting in either tubular steel or aluminum rod such as the famous Blackburn. The aluminum type must have at least six struts with angled bracing at the back. Some riders prefer to carry light loads on day rides in a fanny pack or small daypack. This leaves your bicycle completely unencumbered, and therefore more responsive and lighter. Unfortunately, you will also be hotter.

Fenders are a good idea for commuting but will clog with mud during off road use. Mount stiff plastic sheets at key points on the frame and carrier to deflect mud and water, or make nylon covers for the rear carrier, attached with Velcro.

Panniers for the rear carrier should be narrow enough to clear the cantilever arches and firmly enough mounted to stay attached on the roughest downhill runs. Avoid designs which use springs or shock cords to secure the bags. Kangaroo has a very good design, but most of the others can be modified. There are small bags designed to fit on the handlebars and inside the frame as well.

Choosing equipment without experience is guesswork. Try a brief test ride or a full field trip on a borrowed or rented machine. If possible, obtain information from your local cycle club.

LOOSE SCREWS & FLAT TIRES
BACKCOUNTRY MAINTENANCE

Good quality mountain bikes are tough but so is the sport of backcountry biking. There isn't anything on a mountain bike that cannot be broken or worn out in the course of normal trail riding. You can expect every nut and bolt to rattle loose eventually. Consider that one loose nut can force you to walk if you do not have the tools to tighten it. Tires always seem to go flat when you are the furthest distance from your vehicle.

BICYCLE TOOL KIT

My tool kit is designed to be the lightest kit possible that will enable me to fix all the common problems that happen in the backcountry. My kit weighs 1 kilogram and every tool in it is well used. Put together your own tool kit and don't leave home without it.

Tire patch kit	Check the tube of glue often. Opened tubes tend to dry out.
Tire pump	Keep the pump in some sort of bag - a tube sewn from nylon cloth is ideal. Dirt in the pump will soon render it useless.
Tire pressure	Make sure it covers the range of guage air pressure you use. Some cyclists pump tires up to 90 psi for riding on pavement even when the tire is only rated for 60 psi.
Screw drivers	Slotted and Phillips. An additional small slotted driver is handy for fine tuning derailleur adjustments.
Spare spokes	A broken spoke can cause the tire to rub on the chain stay or forks making the bike very difficult to ride.
Freewheel tools	There are many models of these removal tools. Buy the right one to fit your particular freewheel. If a spoke breaks on the free wheel side of your rear tire, you must remove the freewheel to replace the spoke.
Spoke wrench Crescent wrench	The wrench must fit the freewheel removal tool. The 200 mm Craftsman wrench from Sears has an extra wide span that fits most freewheel removal tools.
Wrenches	8, 9 and 10 mm dogbone wrench. One tool combines 10 box wrenches
Headset wrench	32 mm; Small cheap ones are hard to find. A loose headset will self-destruct from the vibrations.
Allen keys	4,5 and 6 mm
Chain rivet tool	Chains break with no warning. This little gem can put them back together.
Spare chain links	When chains break, there are often some mangled links.
Oil	Ordinary motor oil works just fine. If you want to get fancy, get a graphite motor oil. A sewing machine oiler makes an excellent non-leaking container.
Needle nose pliers	Good for adjusting cables and cutting spokes.
Nylon pouch	The nylon strap around my tool kit serves as a third hand to compress the brakes when I am adjusting the brake cable.
Spare nuts & Bolts	

I don't carry a spare inner tube because they are heavy and in over 125 days of riding I have never known anyone to need one. If you have to patch a tire in a rainstorm, try drying it out with a butane lighter.

BASE CAMP TOOL KIT

It's a good idea to carry a more comprehensive tool kit in the car on weekend trips.

grease	spare inner tube
more oil	spare rear
hand cleaner	derailleur
bottom bracket tools	spare brakepads
crank remover tool	spare cables
head set tools	spare ball bearings
cleaning rags	spare chain
solvent	

file for smoothing chipped chainring teeth

WASHING THE BIKE

Normal cleaning of a mountain bike usually brings howls of disgust from a road bike purist. Don't be shy with the garden hose. The chain in particular needs drastic measures to get the grit out. Spray the hose directly through a dirty chain. Alternate with brushing and liberal application of WD 40 or any spray on lubricant/cleaner.

BROKEN REAR DERAILLEUR

Sooner or later you or someone in your group will trash a rear derailleur. If it is just slightly bent, try bending it back with a crescent wrench or 6mm Allen key placed in the main mounting bolt. If the derailleur is reduced to little bits of metal scattered along the trail, you will have to try something else. If you have horizontal rather than vertical dropouts try this emergency procedure. Remove what's left of the derailleur. Loosen the rear wheel nuts and move the wheel forward in the dropouts. Use the chain rivet tool to shorten the chain so that it fits snugly on an appropriate gear. Tighten the chain by pulling the rear wheel back in the dropouts and securely tighten the wheel nuts. If the chain is tight enough it will stay in the gear you placed it in and you will have a single gear bike that will get you back to the trailhead.

Mountain bikes ridden hard in the backcountry need a complete overhaul at least every 30 days of riding. I have found that derailleurs, chains, brakepads, the small chainring and many bearings all wear out in less than 50 days of hard riding.

OVERHAUL

Most bike shops can quickly and painlessly refurbish your mount. A competent, self reliant backcountry cyclist should be capable of disassembling, cleaning, lubricating, reassembling and adjusting the entire bicycle. There are good hands on courses run through bicycle shops, bicycle clubs, and colleges. Books and friends may also be a help. Learning more about bicycle maintenance will make your steed less intimidating and backcountry biking more enjoyable.

Sealed bearings in mountain bikes can be cleaned and repacked with grease without removing the bearing cartridges from the hubs. Remove the plastic cover from the cartridge carefully with a sharp knife. Use liquid and spray solvents to remove the old grease - pressurized air works best. After drying, pack the cartridge full of a good quality bicycle grease and replace the cover.

A well balanced cyclist with dry feet. ⤵
Jeff Gruttz crossing the Oldman River near Cache Creek.

TECHNIQUE

TAMING YOUR STEED
FAT TIRE RIDING TIPS

Riding technique can be summed up in the statement "hang on, hang loose and let her buck".

HANG ON

One of the most important things uninitiated mountain bike riders have to learn is to stand up while riding out bumps or riding downhill. You have three points of attachment to the bicycle: the handlebars, the pedals and the seat. Standing up helps you hang on to two of them. It is essential to keep weight on the pedals in order to let your shoes maintain a firm grip. Keeping your bum off the seat while riding out a rough spot prevents bucking bronco dismounts where the rear tire hits a bump and bucks you off the seat. While standing up, shift your weight (bum) backwards and grip the seat between your thighs for lateral control of the bike. Standing up lets your knees flex and absorb bumps. Standing up also gives you more power to pedal over obstacles. Keep your pedals roughly parallel to the ground, one to the front and one to the rear, to give you more ground clearance. The flex in the cranks also absorbs shock.

While riding downhill, your hands must be able to hang on to the grips and control the brakes at the same time. Wrap your thumb and forefinger around the handlebar grip and grip the brake with the other three fingers. This lets you apply full brake or no brake and never loosen your grip just in case you ride around a corner and meet a horse in the middle of the trail.

HANG LOOSE

Rigid elbows, knees, waist, and neck will transmit vibrations to your head blurring your vision and thought. Hang loose - be a big shock absorber so your head stays relatively still and your kidneys don't get bruised.

LET HER BUCK

Riding out the bumps on a downhill descent has a lot in common with riding a bucking bronco or mogul skiing. Your steed or your skis go up and down just as your handlebars go up and down. Elbows and knees not only must vibrate to absorb little bumps, they must extend and flex to let the bike ride over the larger variations in terrain and let your body remain relatively still. In mogul skiing, your knees extend and flex to absorb the bumps.

Bracing for a steep descent. Exploring a dirt bike trail on the crest of Cabin Ridge.

More advanced technique involves prejumping - that is trying to move the bike or skis downward or upward before you hit the dip or rise. This compensates for reaction time and let's you "work" the bumps rather than let the bumps "work" you.

GEARING

It is almost impossible to gear down while the chain is under tension. You must gear down before you reach a hill where you need a lower gear. If you are descending into a gully, gear down to the lowest gear before you reach bottom and start to climb the other side.

HILL CLIMBING

Weight can be shifted forward or backward on the bike while climbing a hill. If your weight is too far forward, the back wheel will spin and you will lose your balance and your momentum. If your weight is too far back, the front wheel will rise off the ground. It is more efficient to sit while grinding up a hill. You can always stand if you need more power. Traversing across a hill or even a wide road can decrease the climbing angle significantly.

Climbing hills is hard on knee joints. Pace yourself and don't exceed your optimum training heart rate on a long ride. If the hill is too long, or too steep, or too rough, don't hesitate to get off and walk the bike. On some "terrific" ridge rides you can expect to push the bike uphill for 2 hours or more.

CREEK CROSSINGS

Most backcountry bike rides outside of the National Parks involve crossing unbridged creeks or rivers. Most creeks are shallow enough to ride across. However, on most trips your feet will get wet - the sooner you get used to the idea, the more you will enjoy the sport.

Riding across creeks can be fun, challenging and faster than dismounting and walking across. Sealed bearings will leak if you peddle through enough creeks - carrying your bike across creeks and getting your feet wet will definitely prolong the life of your wheel bearings.

Here is the most successful technique for riding across creeks. Slow down as you approach the creek and put the bike in the lowest gear. Apply the brakes while peddling if necessary to keep tension on the chain. Pick out a route across the smoothest part of the creek bed then peddle as hard as you can just before you reach the water and keep peddling until you fall off or climb out the other side. If you hit the water too fast, the front wheel will invariably bounce off a boulder and knock you off balance. Almost all creeks have large rocks lurking beneath the water waiting to challenge your front tire - these aren't called the Rocky Mountains for nothing.

If you are crossing a creek on a log, be sure to walk the bike on the downstream side of the log. It is very comical to see a bike being dragged under a log by the current.

To ford deeper rivers, it is necessary to carry the bike since a bike has too much drag in the water and tends to get pushed downstream. The bike is of no use as the third leg of a stable tripod formation. If you need a third leg for balance in a fast current, lock arms with a partner or use a stick for support, **but carry the bike.**

RUT RIDING

Many trails have deep ruts left by years of travel by horses, cattle or elk. The body must be shifted side to side to maintain balance and assist steering. Nothing but practice will make you any better at it.

JUMPING LOGS

Most trails have logs across them - jumping the bike across logs saves time and energy. It is a fairly simple technique of pulling up on the handlebars to let the front wheel ride over the log. Your weight is then shifted aggressively forward to unweight the rear wheel and let it ride over the log. Be sure to keep your bum off the seat to avoid a bucking bronco dismount. Jumping logs becomes difficult or dangerous when the log is angled across the trail and the log has a slippery surface. The front wheel tends to slip sideways and dump you onto the log.

BRAIN BUCKETS

The mountains are full of hazards and that is one of the things that keeps them interesting. It never ceases to surprise me how I can fall off the bike on a level trail and hit my head on the ground. Helmets have improved dramatically in recent years and are a wise precaution. If you are one of those people who find them unbearably hot, at least strap your brain bucket onto the bike for the long push and grind uphill and wear it on the descent.

DISMOUNTS

Sooner or later everyone loses control of the bike and crashes. Landing gracefully and painlessly is a valuable skill. The safest and most graceful way to crash is to drop the bike and run - I call it the paratrooper dismount because a paratrooper always lands on his feet. To do a paratrooper dismount, you need to be able to get your feet clear of the peddles which is difficult to do if you are using toeclips. When you realize that you are losing control of the bike, push down on the handlebars and raise your knees to your chin so that your feet clear the top tube and then land on the run - you will have several microseconds to think about it. If you stay on your feet you have done a successful paratrooper dismount. If you trip and do cartwheels or somersaults you will have entertained your friends with a Chinese circus dismount, definitely a hazardous procedure. Always wear cycling gloves while backcountry biking just in case you do a Chinese circus dismount and your hands hit the dirt.

Some people have the habit of going down with the bike, a captain-of-the-ship dismount. I have always thought that during a crash the most dangerous object around me is the bike. In a crash I always try to push away from the bike but that is not always possible. If the front wheel drops into a hole or hits a rock and turns sideways, the rider can do an involuntary handstand on the handlebars and go down with the bike just like a captain going down with his ship. If this happens the best you can do is tuck in your head, roll on one shoulder and hope that all you damage is your ego.

An alloy horse at Chaba River Warden Cabin near the Athabasca River. ➪ Winston Churchill Range in the background.

ETHICS

DEBATING ABOUT BICYCLES
IN THE BACKCOUNTRY

Mountain bike travel in the backcountry has been a controversial topic and is only now being accepted as a legitimate activity in parks and forest areas. I promote the sport of backcountry biking with a clear conscience. I want wilderness areas to mean more to people than a shaded area on a map and a good idea. Personal experience of natural areas through cycling and other activities builds appreciation and involvement that is essential for the protection of these areas at public expense.

Many people have argued that mountain bikes can erode trails and cause environmental damage. No comprehensive scientific studies have been done but park managers and cyclists have the benefit of several years of experience observing the effects of mountain bike use on trails. It is necessary to keep in mind the difference between a bicycle's potential to cause damage and the actual observed effect. The consensus of park managers in the National Parks and Kananaskis Country is that there has been no evidence of significant trail degradation contributable to mountain bikes and that it is not an important issue.

The impact of bikes on a trail is comparable to that of hiking. Any differences are academic. The trail impact is far less than that of horses, cattle or elk, at least one of which frequents all of the trails in this book. People who propose that mountain bikes cause significant trail damage may be acting out of a personal bias against bicycles rather than being realistic and objective.

Opponents of mountain bikes have argued that they are mechanical and therefore inappropriate in natural areas.

Backpacking gas stoves, internal frame packs, carbon fiber kayaks, two way radios and helicopters are also mechanical items used to enhance people's enjoyment of the wilderness.

There is always opposition to new forms of recreation that are not part of the traditions of that era. Some of the arguments against cross country skiing when it was first introduced in the Rockies would now seem foreign to us. The traditional campfire and teepee supported by the liberal use of an axe, have been largely replaced by gas stoves and nylon tents. Traditional hunting and gathering have been replaced by lightweight pack-in foods. There has been a trend toward low impact use of the wilderness. Traditional use patterns give way to better ways of doing things, which eventually become traditions themselves.

Opponents of backcountry biking have confused mountain bikes with motorized dirt bikes. The destructive power of a motorized dirt bike comes from the tremendous torque on the rear wheel supplied by the power of a gasoline engine. The torque on a bicycle wheel is limited by the strength, energy and balance of a human being. "Self-propelled" would be a better way of characterizing backcountry bicycle travel. Self-propelled forms of travel such as hiking, cross country skiing, canoeing and cycling require physical effort by the participant. The range of travel and erosion power is limited by the input of human energy. Horses, like motorized vehicles, have the potential to do much more damage to the environment.

Some of the people opposed to backcountry bicycle travel are horseback riders.

Some of them fail to realize that they are living in a glass house. Horse travel in wilderness areas is not without problems. Trail erosion, feral horses, conflict with hikers, unsightly smelly droppings, destruction of vegetation through grazing and introduction of non-native plants through hay and feed and injury or abandonment of the horse riders are among the problems. In many ways, bicycle travel is more conducive to enjoying wilderness areas. I am not opposed to horseback riding in wilderness areas. I merely wish to keep the pros and cons of horse and bicycle travel in perspective. Many people I have spoken to, including horseback riders, hikers and members of the Alberta Wilderness Association are of the opinion that bicycles should be allowed access to all of the areas that horses are allowed access to.

Although bicycles can be very useful for travel on abandoned roads and the smoother trails in parks, their range of usefulness is limited. Many of the trails in the National Parks are narrow, deeply rutted, or steep. Few people have any interest in cycling any distance on such trails. Even if there were no restrictions, most hiking trails in the parks would seldom if ever be travelled by bicycles. There are other trails such as Ribbon Creek trail and the Upper Lake trail in Kananaskis and interpretive trails where bicycles can conflict with hikers and may not be appropriate.

Opponents of mountain bikes have stated that "Outside the National Parks and Forest Land Use Zone areas, the vast majority of lands lie available for the gamut of uses Albertans desire", which suggests that bicycles should be subject to the same restrictions as motorized vehicles. In the case of backcountry biking, this is nothing more than an attempt to evade the issue. This argument is meaningful for some activities such as four-wheel driving or racing, where the activity itself is more important than the environment it takes place in. The issue at hand is enjoyment of wilderness areas, the National Parks, Forest Land Use Zones and the Eastern Slopes. Wilderness is a limited commodity. In order to be supported at public expense, it must be enjoyed or at least be meaningful to the public. I believe that bicycling, both on roads and trails is a very appropriate way for the public to experience parks and other protected areas.

THE GREAT OUTDOORS
IT'S THERE TO SHARE

AT THE EDGE

The development of the mountain bike has opened up exciting recreational opportunities which complement other backcountry activities such as hiking, climbing and appreciation of wild areas. We are all pioneering a new sport. Park managers, however, are questioning the appropriateness of this form of backcountry travel. There is concern over environmental and social values. Your freedom to cycle trails could be seriously affected by complaints from hikers, evacuation of stranded cyclists at public expense or trampled vegetation.

Because the behavior and attitude of backcountry cyclists will affect the future of the sport, consideration of other trail users is essential for the continued acceptance and development of this sport.

The Code of Ethics opposite has been approved and adopted by the Elbow Valley Cycle Club of Calgary, Alberta.

1 WATCH FOR OTHERS ON THE TRAIL

When riding downhill, watch carefully for hikers and horses. Approach corners and blind spots in anticipation of surprising someone. Being sensitive to how others perceive you, will help to build a positive image for your sport and decrease the concerns about sharing the trails with bicycles.

2 CONTROL YOUR SPEED

Your skill as a rider and the terrain determine safe speeds.

3 PASS WITH CARE

The cyclist bears the burden of responsibility to make the passing go smoothly.

When Passing Horses
- It is usually best to get off the bike and walk.
- Speak a friendly word of greeting to reassure both horse and rider.
- To give a horse room to pass, it may be necessary to step off the trail. If practical, move to the lower side of the trail. Horses feel less threatened by a lower object.
- Be especially careful when passing pack horses. They tend to be more skittish than a horse controlled by a rider.

When Passing Hikers
- Use a bell and give adequate warning to prevent startling hikers. Being jolted from a state of serenity by a passing bicycle can arouse the wrath of the most tolerant hiker.

4 STAY ON THE TRAILS

Riding off the trails, especially in meadows, can damage vegetation and leave unsightly tire tracks.

5 DO NOT HARASS WILDLIFE OR LIVESTOCK

Keep a safe distance from animals and give them time to move off of the trail. Even approaching wildlife with a camera can constitute harassment.

6 DON'T LITTER

Pack out what you pack in. Carry out more than your share if you have room in your bags.

7 BE PREPARED FOR MECHANICAL PROBLEMS

Carry a tool kit on backcountry rides. Knobby tires do go flat. A single loose nut can mean a disabled bicycle. A bicycle can take you into the backcountry further than you can walk out in a day. As a responsible cyclist, make sure you get back under your own power.

8 PLAN AHEAD

Make sure cycle routes are within your ability and time limitations.

Check:

Trail conditions   Land ownership
Closures   Weather forecasts   Permits
Campsite locations   Potential hazards

9 MINIMIZE ENVIRONMENTAL IMPACT

Wait for trails to dry out in the spring before you ride them. Riding wet muddy trails is hard on the bike and hard on the trails. Dry trails are much more enjoyable.

10 MINIMIZE SOCIAL IMPACT

Select trails which are suitable for backcountry cycling. Avoiding high use areas will increase your enjoyment of the sport.

BICYCLES AND HORSES SHARING THE TRAILS

Many of the trails used for backcountry biking are also used for recreational horseback riding. There is a strong tradition of horse travel in the Canadian Rockies. Traditions change, but they also deserve to be respected. The trail systems in the Sheep and Elbow valleys in particular were developed primarily for recreational horseback travel, and if cyclists want to ride these trails they must be willing to share them with horses.

GETTING ACQUAINTED

I spent a weekend riding my mountain bike with Judy and Linda, members of the Calgary Regional Competitive Trail Riders, an equestrian club. Marg, the ride chairman for the 1986 Calgary Regional competitive trail ride had asked me for some help in measuring the length of the trails for next summer's ride. Horses don't have odometers but bicycles do. Would I help? Of course I would - it was an excellent opportunity to learn more about how cyclists and horse riders interact on the trails.

We spent two days riding together near the North Fork Equestrian Area in Kananaskis Country. The bicycle was a new experience for the horses, Quincy and Chamois. They were accustomed to motorbikes, but this bike was almost silent except for the whir of the chain and slapping of the panniers. At first, the horses' eyes bugged out and their ears went forward, but after several kilometres they learned to accept the bicycle. Being competitive animals, they wanted to chase the bike and pass it.

TRAIL PREFERENCES MUD OR ROCKS?

The weekend held a few surprises for Judy and Linda. They learned that I didn't like to cycle their favorite trails. A good horse trail has a soft surface that provides some cushion to a horse's hooves. A little mud is just fine - the horses know how to slide in it. Mud on a bike is like sand in a gear box. When the trails are muddy I haul out the windsurfer or work on my yard; anything but mountain biking. A good mountain bike trail has a hard stony surface, or at least a dry surface. Horses tend to stumble among rocks, but a few boulders are no problem to a bike. In New Zealand they are called "push bikes" - if the going gets to rough, you get off and push. They were also surprised at how a mountain bike could go down a steep hill without skidding. The fat knobby tires provide tremendous traction and the cantilever brakes provide extraordinary braking power. They have to, - skidding the tires often means falling off the bike or at least losing momentum while climbing a hill.

Horses can be coaxed up steep and hair-raising trails. However, it was becoming obvious that horses were designed as a flat land animal. With two thirds of their weight on their front feet, going down a steep hill is an invitation to do a somersault.

Neither cyclists nor horseback riders like rutted trails crossed with tree roots. Horses tend to trip on the roots and loose their balance in the ruts. The Sheep and Elbow valleys offer much better equestrian trails than Banff National Park where years of hard use by commercial horse outfitters on soft, wet soils has created deeply rutted trails. Judy and Linda also discovered that a bike usually covers more trail in a day than a horse. On the second day of riding we covered 18 kilometres at a pace of 4 km per hour over hilly ground. Judy traded the three year old mare, Chamois, for an older horse, saying that the ride was too much for a horse as young as Chamois regardless of her conditioning. With my bike, I travel as slow as 5 km per hour when walking the bike over rough ground and as fast as 15 km per hour on a gravel road. On a moderately steep road it is not uncommon for a bike to reach peak speeds of 40 km per hour.

My bicycle is more easily transported than a horse. I load it on the bike rack and drive to one of the trailheads scattered throughout the mountains. I ride long loop trips on relatively stony ground where the horse riders seldom travel.

I was finding answers to some questions that had been puzzling me. In two summers of riding the equestrian trails in the Sheep and Elbow valleys of Kananaskis Country, I had met very few horses on the trails - 12 horses in 30 days of cycling. Yet the rangers told me that the equestrian use had doubled to 300 rider days per weekend in the Sheep and Elbow valleys. There are several reasons for the lack of contact. Very few of the horseback riders in the Sheep and Elbow valleys venture out on the 20 to 70 km loop trips that I usually cover on the bike. They prefer shorter, one to three hour loop trips that start at camp. Loading the horses in a trailer to go to a distant trailhead is a chore they avoid.

Horse riders and cyclists have different preferences in trails. Terrain and transportation considerations tend to separate horse and bicycle activity. Some trails in the eastern slopes already have more bicycle traffic than horse traffic, while other trails have never seen a cyclist. Many of the better horse trails will never be attractive for cycling. Death Valley and 9999 trails are too wet and bumpy to be attractive cycling trails. On the other hand, the Little Elbow and the Sheep River trails are too long and rocky to be popular horse trails. So it seems that the best backcountry bicycle trails fit into a recreational void between the steep hiking trails along the Divide and the more gentle, muddy horse trails in the foothills.

The horse riders were almost unanimous in their praise of the trail system and camps created by the Alberta Forestry Service. The one improvement they all wanted to see was more short loop trails that start and end at the four equestrian camps: Ford Creek, North Fork, Sandy McNabb and Bluerock.

MEETING ON THE TRAILS

When horse riders and cyclists meet on a trail, the cyclist bears the burden of the responsibility to make the passing go smoothly. The cyclist must always be watching for horses on the trail, especially while riding downhill. If the horse and cyclist are travelling in opposite directions, the cyclist should dismount and walk the bike off the trail. This reassures both horse and rider. A horse feels less threatened by a strange object if it is on the lower side of the trail. Like Judy told me: "Horses are basically chicken. If a horse sees something above it, it is afraid that it might jump on top of it. At one stage in the evolution of horses they were three feet tall and lived among sabretooth tigers." Horses can be spooked by bicycles or any unfamiliar object.

Bicycles usually travel faster than horses. When a bicycle is overtaking a horse, the rider can help by letting the cyclist pass.

I got more surprises on a bicycle trip in Willmore Wilderness. The horses there were even less accustomed to the sight of a bicycle, especially pack horses which are more skittish than a horse controlled by a rider. Passing horses, I noticed, got upset when I left my bike at the side of the trail and walked away from it, but were much calmer when I stayed with the bike. My friend Judy enlightened me once again: "If a horse sees that you don't want to be near some strange object, why should he be brave enough to get close to it?" On another occasion I stood near my bike and a horse refused to pass me. The frustrated rider said "Will you speak - he doesn't know what you are until he hears you speak". A friendly word of greeting improved my relations with both the horse and the rider.

THE POOR MAN'S HORSE

The fat tire klunkers we rode when we were kids have been reincarnated. The development of the mountain bike has extended cycling onto backcountry trails and former tedious hikes down fire roads and logging roads have now become interesting bicycle trips. Similarly, seismic lines which have been regarded by some as scars upon the land are now regarded by the same people as important recreational resources. The mountain bike has become the poor man's horse. I am pleased that horse riders have been so willing to share the trails with bicycles.

I extend a special thank you to Judy, Marg and Linda. They say that I'm getting more "horsey". The last time I was talking to Linda, she was shopping around for a mountain bike!

"Bull Moose" handlebars. on Wolf Creek trail.
From left to right: Colynn Kerr, Sheryle Elliot.

INTRODUCTION
TO THE TRAILS

READ THIS FIRST

GEOGRAPHY COVERED

This guide covers selected trails in:
- Jasper National Park
- Banff National Park
- Yoho National Park
- Kootenay National Park
- Waterton National Park
- Kananaskis Country
- Crowsnest River Drainage
- Castle River Drainage

And trails which lead in to Mount Assiniboine Provincial Park and Elk Lakes Provincial Park on the British Columbia side of the Rockies

All but four short sections of trail in this guide were explored by the author who travelled all but a few by mountain bike. It has been our intention to provide first hand information on cycling conditions not available elsewhere. Some people are looking for a "sure thing" while others prefer the new and unexplored. There are many more good bicycle routes to explore in the Rockies, particularly in southern Alberta and on the western side of the Divide in British Columbia.

NATIONAL PARKS DESIGNATED TRAILS

Parks Canada has designated trails for use by mountain bikes in the National Parks.

It is illegal to cycle off road anywhere in the National Parks other than on designated trails.

Parks Canada has heard the viewpoints of both the pro-mountain biking and anti-mountain biking lobbies, and although they recognize the positive values and recreational potential of backcountry bicycling, they do have legitimate concerns over trail user conflicts. Parks Canada must balance the interests of cyclists, hikers and horseback riders. This guidebook, therefore, is based on the trails designated by Parks Canada for backcountry bicycling in 1986. The following trails (not described) were added in 1987:

- Alexandra Road - 26.4 km
- Saskatchewan Road - 4.0 km
- Sarbach Road - 5.0 km
- Chateau Lake Louise to Moraine Lake 12.9 km on old trail.
- Banff & Lake Louise townsite trails

Check with a Parks Canada information office for the latest list of designated trails.

WEATHER & SEASONS

Peak river flow in the Rockies occurs in mid-June as the dense snowpack in the high country melts. Rivers that are thigh-high and fast flowing in June may be knee-high and relatively easy to cross in July and August. Water levels in the book are given for summer conditions in July and August. Many rivers, especially the Highwood, may be too high for you to cross in June.

No matter how hot and sunny the weather is when you start out in the morning, take a rainjacket and an extra layer of insulation. The weather in the Rockies is practiced in the art of deception. It can rain or snow on you when you least expect it. In June, July and August, most days are warm enough to ride wearing shorts and a T shirt or no shirt at all. The strong summer sunshine makes sunscreen standard equipment. The temperature can drop quickly in the mountain environment and frost is not uncommon at night, even after a warm day.

Some of the trails described as gravel roads may be rideable as early as May, but most trails are not snow free and dry until June. Resist the temptation to start riding trails too early in the season. Riding muddy trails is not much fun and can cause trail erosion. High country rides should be undertaken in July and August. Weather and trail conditions vary from season to season and in unpredictable fall months can be either cold and snowy or warm and sunny. The conditions on a trail can change dramatically during the season. A trail surface that is wet and muddy in the fall and spring can become pitted with the hooves of elk, cattle or horses. The trail may be quite rough in early summer but as the trail surface dries out, it becomes weak and crumbly - the passage of anything on feet, hooves or wheels breaks up the surface and smooths it out. Trails that are rough in June can be pleasantly smooth by August.

The seasons progress at different rates on north and south slopes. South facing slopes may be firm and dry in May while the north slopes are still knee deep in snow. Different soil and wetter conditions on north slopes makes them less enjoyable to ride even in midsummer.

DRINKING WATER

Drinking water is of special concern to backcountry cyclists because they drink a lot of it. Many of the trails are in valley bottoms where the water is more likely to be contaminated. Especially in the foothills where most streams are shared with cattle, there is a possibility of becoming infected with *giardia lamblia,* a protozoan that causes diarrhea, nausea, severe stomach cramps and listlessness. The main infective strain is most commonly found in domestic dogs, humans and beaver, hence the name "beaver fever". The organism enters waterways through the feces of these animals.

Always start a backcountry cycling trip with a full water bottle. Collect drinking water from small springs and creeks - larger waterways receive water from a larger watershed and are more likely to be contaminated. We have drank water from almost every route in this guide with no ill effects. Does that mean that the water is safe, that we are immune to *giardia* or that we are just lucky? I'm not really sure.

TRAIL MUNCHIES

Vast amounts of energy can be expended on a backcountry bicycle tour. Be sure to pack some high energy foods such as chocolate, raisins, fruit or baked goods - it's an excellent way to win friends and influence people. Fruit has a much better chance of surviving a banana mashing trail if it is packed in a plastic container with some padding around it.

GETTING YOUR OATS

By popular demand I have included the recipe for one of the most popular foods to ever be pulled out of a pannier. They have never failed to please.

Mix the dry ingredients in one bowl and the wet ingredients in another bowl and then mix them all together.

PEANUT POLKA DOTTIES

Preheat oven to 175 Celsius (350 F).
500 ml quick cooking oats
2 ml salt
200 ml large chocolate chips
300 ml canned sweetened condensed milk
100 ml peanut butter
5 ml vanilla
30 ml water

USING THIS BOOK

MAPS

Maps are used in this guide to graphically display trails and communicate most of the route finding information. Detailed route finding directions were intentionally avoided except when the route is ambiguous or difficult to find. Elevations are indicated on the maps at the high points and low points along the trail. These help to indicate the ascents and descents and steepness of the grade.

Distances are indicated on the maps between key points. The majority were measured with either a mechanical or electronic odometer on a mountain bike. Some distances were estimated from topographical maps.

Trail access information is intended to be detailed enough so you can find the trailhead using only a road map.

LEGEND

road		steep uphill	
biking trail	🚵	ford	🚵
hiking trail	🚶	horses	🐎
powerline	—•—•—	bridge	⌣
seismic line	– – –	distances	•▬▬•
park boundary	–•–•–	elevations	1370m
campground	⋀	town	O
picnic area	🛆	mountain	▲
warden cabin	🏠	lookout/hill	△
meadow	🌿	sawmill sites	◆
viewpoint	👓	parking	P
waterfall	🏔	gates, gas wells, microwave tower	X
reccommended direction of travel	→		

TOPOGRAPHICAL MAPS

The maps in the book are not intended as substitutes for topographical maps. National Topographical System (NTS) maps can provide a wealth of information about a landscape and may be necessary for route finding on some of the more remote and less developed trails. Reading topographical maps, like reading a book, is a skill that needs to be practiced and developed. Many of the trails in the guide are not marked on the topographical maps, especially the newer trails in the Sheep Valley and Elbow Valley. I find that he NTS maps are not very reliable in indicating whether a route is a trail or a road. Generally, there are many more roads than the maps indicate. The maps in this guide provide information not available on many of the topographical maps and provide a valuable compliment to them. National Topographical System maps may be obtained from local map dealers, from park information offices or may be mail ordered from:

Canada Map Office
Surveys and Mapping Branch
Department of Energy, Mines and Resources
Ottawa, Canada K1A 0E9.

PARKS MAPS

Most of the trails in the National Parks and Kananaskis Country are marked and signed and easy to follow. Both Parks Canada and Kananaskis Country have produced excellent topographical maps that combine several sheets from the National Topographical System.

28

HIKING

This guide is intended to compliment the hiking trail guides, not replace them. There are many places where a mountain bike can be used on old roads to gain access to trails that are more suitable for hiking than cycling. I have mentioned many hiking trails in this guide that are accessible from the cycling routes. Consult the appropriate hiking trail guides for more details.

Kananaskis Country Trail Guide, *Gillean Daffern,* Rocky Mountain Books 2nd ed 1985
The Canadian Rockies Trail Guide, *Patton & Robinson,* Summerthought 3rd ed 1986
Hiking Alberta's Southwest, *Joey Ambrosi,* Douglas & McIntyre, 1st ed 1984

ROADS

Fire
Logging
Seismic Exploration
Gass Well Access
Grazing Land Access
Four-Wheel Drive

To describe the quality of the roads and standardize the terminology, I have described them as high grade, smooth, good, rough, or very rough. The surface has been described as either gravel or dirt. Gravel refers either to gravel added during construction of the road or a naturally stony, well drained surface.

Many trails have been described as "vegetated" referring to grasses, sedges, herbaceous plants, mosses or shrubs growing on the trail surface. The very best trail surface is a well drained sandy or shale soil covered with pine needles.

Colynn Kerr fording the West Fork of the Little Elbow River near Mount Romulus campground.

TRAVELLING TIME

Trails can be travelled much more quickly on a mountain bike than on foot or on horseback. Travel times vary from 5 to 15 kilometres per hour and from 30 to 60 minutes for each 300 metres of elevation gained. Allow extra time for socializing, loafing, birdwatching, looking for the Lost Lemon Gold Mine or whatever else you came for.

All of the trails in the book can be ridden as day trips. There are campgrounds throughout the Canadian Rockies that can serve as base camps for day trips. If you are planning an overnight trip, keep in mind that a mountain bike becomes unmanageable on a rough trail when it is weighed down with camping gear. The best trails for overnight trips are listed below.

Colynn Kerr & Gerhardt Lepp sinking in "quick mud" on the Castle River road.

1	Snake Indian Falls
9	Whirlpool River - Moab Lake
10	Fryatt Creek
11	Athabasca River
13	Amiskwi River Fire Road
15	Blaeberry River Road
16	Ottertail River Fire Road
17	Ice River Road - Crozier Loop
18	Crozier Road
23	Ya Ha Tinda to Scotch Camp
26	Cascade Fire Road
31	Bryant Creek
32	Spray River Fire Road
44	Evan-Thomas Creek
49	Elk Pass to Elk Lakes
60	Quirk Creek - Wildhorse Loop
62	Elbow Loop
70	Sheep River
73	Odlum Pond
84	Salter Creek - Willow Creek
91	Headwaters of the Oldman R.
101	Daisy Creek
106	Castle River
108	Akamina - Kishinena

TENDER, TOUGH, TERRIFIC

Trails vary widely in their difficulty. The trails in this book have been rated as Tender, Tough and Terrific, similar to the rating for ski slopes: Easiest, More Difficult, Most Difficult. The dominant factors considered in the rating of each trail are slope, elevation gain, and trail surface. These factors affect the skill level required to safely ride the trail and the amount of energy expended. The ratings are subjective and you may not agree with my idea of what is easy. However, I have tried to make the ratings consistent.

Distance was intentionally not included in the rating of difficulty. The distance is included separately in the beginning of each trail description. The elevation gain and other comments in the trail description should also be considered in your own evaluation of the difficulty of the ride.

If you are new to the sport and your derriere is prone to saddle sores, try a "Tender" trail until you are "Tough" enough. "Terrific" trails are usually a long, hard push up to a ridge. The feeling of gazing down upon the world from a mountain ridge and the ride down can be simply terrific. With practice you can develop considerable skill in using topo maps to evaluate slopes and other terrain factors that affect the difficulty of the trails.

The following table summarizes what you can expect on each grade of trail. One or more of the factors may account for the trail rating.

	Tender	Tough	Terrific
Surface	Smooth	Rough spots	Very rough spots
Slope	Little pushing	Some pushing	Up to 20% of distance pushing
Height Gain	Up to 400 m	200 - 600 m	Over 500 m
Fords	Shallow	Knee deep	Thigh deep or fast water
Touring Bike Test	Can ride a touring bike	Touring bike not recommended	Eats bikes

31

SHOT AT, SWORN AT, AND LOST IN A SNOW STORM

Things can go wrong, despite your best intentions. One memorable day in late September, I rode the Threepoint Mountain trail with my friend, Jeff Grutz. That was the day we got shot at, sworn at and lost in a snow storm.

We set out to see if there is a trail along the upper part of Threepoint Creek - there isn't. Despite our efforts to be friendly and not spook his horses, a hunter on horseback told us that he was going to wrap our bikes around our necks. I have deleted his expletives. Later in the day as we dragged our bikes across scree slopes and through canyons along Three-point Creek, it started to snow. With the deep fluffy stuff piling up, we pushed our bikes out to Volcano Ridge trail and up what we thought was Wildhorse trail. It is amazing how places look different under a blanket of snow.

We heard shooting ahead so we put on our brightest clothing and yelled and rang our bells. Unknown to us, a hunter had set up his camp on one side of the trail and set up a practice target on the other side of the trail. We stumbled in between the two. A shot rang out - I felt the shock waves and heard the bullet hit the snow in front of me. The hunter finally heard us after a fit of yelling and cursing. Heated words were exchanged and the hunter finally humiliated us by informing us that we were lost; the Wild-horse trail was still three kilometres to the east. By this time it was getting dark and was snowing hard.

I hope your next ride is less eventful.

JASPER PARK

1 Map 5
SNAKE INDIAN FALLS

Cycling provides access to Snake Indian Falls in one day wheras hiking to Snake Indian Falls and back requires a 2 - 3 day backpacking trip on a very tedious road. Most of the road is enclosed in the trees and there is little view. This trip covers the first leg of the The North Boundary trail, a 150 km hiking trail that wanders up the Snake Indian River, over Snake Indian Pass and on to Mount Robson Provincial Park.

This restricted access dirt and gravel road had been graded a few days before we cycled it and offered smooth easy cycling. Because of the length of this trip, most riders will prefer to push up some of the hills.

The Shale Banks provide a welcome half-way break. Best seen from the 300 m side trails to the warden cabin or the campsite, these 120 m-high black shale banks are topped by trees that tumble into the river as the cliff erodes. A natural mineral lick attracts sheep and goats.

Snake Indian Falls is a large, powerful waterfall which has eroded a long steep canyon on the slow journey to its present site. It's a great spot for lunch and a nap before the long cycle back to the trailhead.

RATING
Tender
DISTANCE
23.1 km one way
TIME
5 - 8 hours return
ELEVATION GAIN
210 m (690 ft)
MAPS
83 E/1 Snaring
83 E/8 Rock Lake

ACCESS
Getting to the start of this trail is half the adventure of the trip. The Snaring Road branches off the west side of Highway 16 10 km east of Jasper. The first 14.2 km of the Snaring Road is a two-way road becoming one-way for the last 19.5 km because of the narrow, cliff hanging sections and blind corners. The permitted direction of travel changes according to a time schedule. Check with the parks information office in Jasper the day before heading out in order to find out the times.

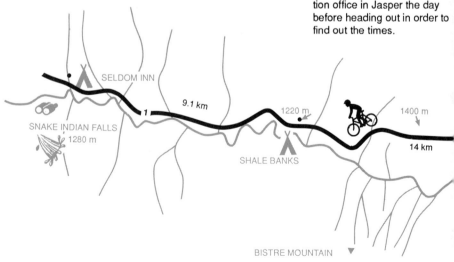

SELDOM INN

9.1 km

1220 m

1400 m

1

SNAKE INDIAN FALLS
1280 m

14 km

SHALE BANKS

BISTRE MOUNTAIN

DE SMET RANGE

2 Map 5
DEVONA LOOKOUT & CELESTINE LAKE

This is a short, interesting trip on a good gravel road to a viewpoint. The road is not too steep to be cycled all the way to the top. The fire lookout has been removed and all that remains is a white lawn chair, a fine perch from which to admire the view of Jasper Lake, Talbot Lake and Roche Miette. It is a fun ride back down the road on a soft carpet of pine needles.

The picnic area at Celestine Lake has the feel of a party after everyone has gone home. This well worn spot was used much more when it was possible to drive all the way to the lake. The long drive along the Celestine Lake Road, an alternating one-way road with narrow, exposed sections maintains the remoteness of the area. Celestine Lake is known for good rainbow trout fishing.

RATING
Tough
DISTANCE
5.0 km one way
TIME
1 - 2 hours return
ELEVATION GAIN
150 m (500 ft)
MAP
82 E/1 Snaring

ACCESS
Getting to the start of this trail is half the adventure of the trip. The Snaring Road branches off the west side of Highway 16, 10 km east of Jasper. The first 14.2 km of the Snaring Road is a two-way road becoming one-way for the last 19.5 km because of the narrow, cliff hanging sections and blind corners. The permitted direction of travel changes according to a time schedule. Check with the parks information office in Jasper the day before heading out to find out the times. The trail starts at a gate on the north-east side of the Celestine Lake parking area.

MAP 5

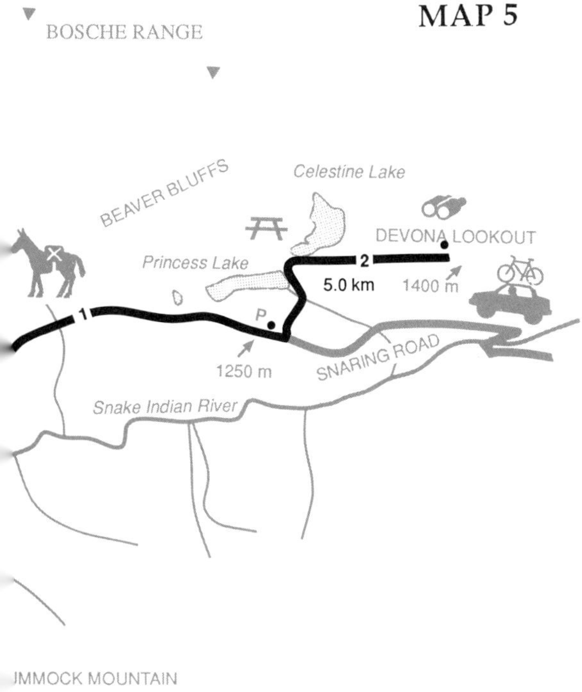

BOSCHE RANGE

BEAVER BLUFFS

Celestine Lake

Princess Lake

DEVONA LOOKOUT

2

5.0 km   1400 m

1

P.

1250 m

SNARING ROAD

Snake Indian River

JMMOCK MOUNTAIN

3 Map 6
BALD HILLS LOOKOUT

Although the Bald Hills Lookout has been removed, a smooth gravel road still leads up the hill to the alpine meadows. If your gears are low enough and your legs are strong enough, you'll be able to pedal most of the way up this hill, but be prepared to walk anyway. Fill your water bottle at the parking lot since you may not find any water on the way up.

The pine forest on the lower part of the hill bears many signs of a recent fire. Numerous pine seedlings poke through the thick carpet of grouse berries. The road rises quickly through a zone of spruce into the subalpine fir and krumholtz, then continues for another 0.5 km into the meadow past the lookout.

The fine view provides ample reward for the uphill grind. The blue-green waters of Maligne Lake stretch south-east toward Samson Narrows. Beyond the lake, Leah Peak and Samson Peak dominate the Queen Elizabeth Range. Mount Unwin and Mount Charlton are the glaciated peaks to the south. The trail through the meadows beckons you to hide your bike and wander to the top of the hill.

The ride down takes a fraction of the time spent coming up. Be considerate of hikers. Test your brakes before starting this trip or you may be in for a big surprise!

RATING
Tough
DISTANCE
5.2 km one way
TIME
2 hours up - 20 minutes down
ELEVATION GAIN
490 m (1600 ft)
MAP
83 C/12 Athabasca Falls

ACCESS
The Maligne Lake Road leaves Highway 16, 2.8 km south of Jasper. Follow the road south-east to Maligne Lake. The right fork at the lake leads to a parking lot at the end of the road 46.4 km from Highway 16. The trailhead is the gated road on the south side of the parking lot.

MAP 6

4 Map 7
SUMMIT LAKES

The short 5 km cycle to South Summit Lake is along a narrow road with a smooth, hard-packed surface. The lovely peaceful surroundings and easy cycling make this the perfect trip for a lazy day.

The first feature of interest is Beaver Lake, only 2.0 km from the trailhead. Steep, grey slabs of limestone in the Queen Elizabeth Range tower over it's blue green waters. The road ends at South Summit Lake. The trail beyond is is narrow, rutted, crossed by roots and quite unsuitable for anything with wheels.

The two Summit Lakes straddle a drainage divide. It is difficult to tell which way they flow because there is no visible outlet. Like Medicine Lake, they are sink lakes which drain through subterranean channels. Sirdar is the imposing mountain beyond the lakes. It was probably named after Field Marshall Lord Kitchener (1850 - 1916) who was made "sirdar" or commander of the Egyptian Army.

RATING
Tender
DISTANCE
5.0 km to South Summit Lake
TIME
2 hours round trip
ELEVATION GAIN
100 m (30 m)
MAP
83 C/13 Medicine Lake

ACCESS
The Maligne Lake Road leaves Highway 16, 2.8 km north of Jasper. Drive up the Maligne Lake Road for 30 km to a small picnic area on the north-east corner of Medicine Lake. The trail starts at a gated road in the picnic area.

HIKING OPTION
JACQUES LAKE
Cycling to the the end of the road at South Summit Lake and then hiking 6.2 km makes a day trip to Jacques Lake feasible.

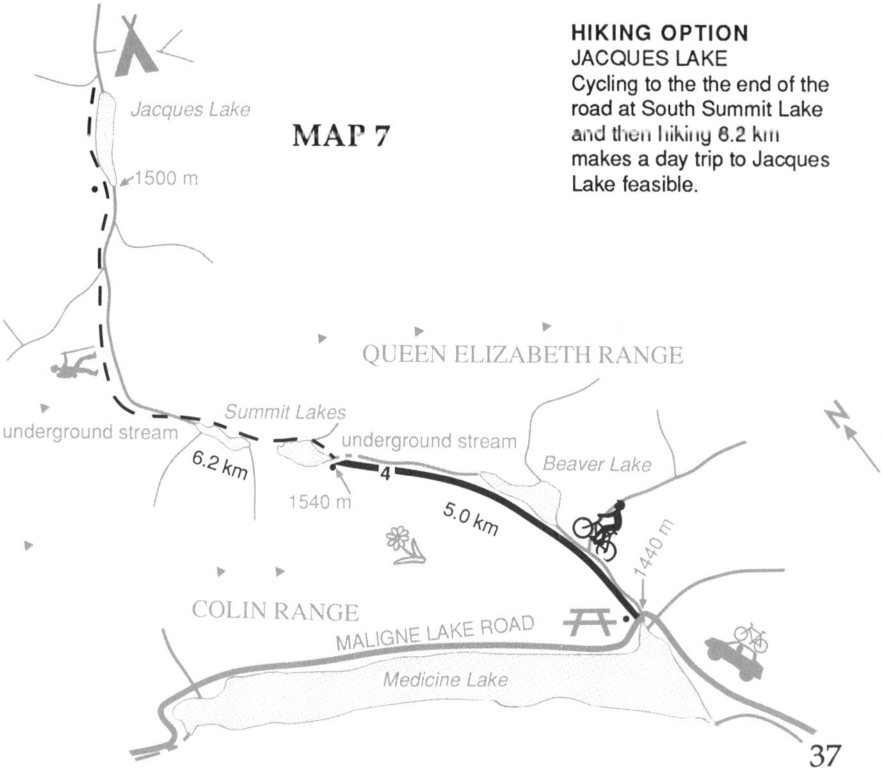

Jacques Lake

MAP 7

1500 m

QUEEN ELIZABETH RANGE

Summit Lakes

underground stream

underground stream

Beaver Lake

6.2 km

1540 m

4

5.0 km

1440 m

COLIN RANGE

MALIGNE LAKE ROAD

Medicine Lake

5 Map 8
SATURDAY NIGHT LAKE

The road to Cabin Lake is smooth riding. The trail beyond is a demanding but enjoyable sidecut horse trail with hills, roots and rocks and smooth sandy sections. Some pushing is required.

The trail traverses the hillside above Cabin Lake, the source of the town's water supply. No boats or canoes are allowed - it is too far to portage from Jasper anyway. The Whistlers make a striking backdrop even though scarred by an aerial tramway. The forest hereabouts is largely Douglas fir with many trees approaching one metre in diameter.

RATING
Tough
DISTANCE
9.4 km one way
TIME
3 - 5 hours round trip
ELEVATION GAIN
300 m (1000 feet)
MAP
83 D/16 Jasper

ACCESS
From Pyramid Avenue, near the Jasper community center, follow Pyramid Lake Drive north toward Pyramid Lake for 2 km. The trail starts where the unmarked and gated Cabin Lake road branches off Pyramid Lake Drive to the west.

Jo-Ann Draper looks out across Cabin Lake to the Whistlers.

Careless campers have left their mark at Saturday Night Lake where a campfire has burned its way into the deep duff layers on the forest floor. The mountain Cairngorm rises beyond the lake. Listen for marmots shrieking in a rock pile near the turnoff.

For an optional route on the return trip, cross the dam on Cabin Lake. This downgraded road goes past a reservoir pumping station to the trailer court on the west side of town.

CYCLING OPTION

The main trail beyond the turnoff to Saturday Night Lake becomes rough and boggy. It's not recommended unless you want to donate some blood to the mosquitoes. The entire Saturday Night Loop of 32 km has been used as a mountain bike race course. Course times of under 3 hours are common, but it's an exercise in masochism.

MAP 8

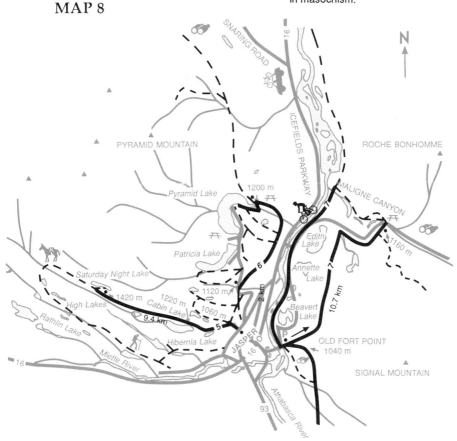

6 Map 8
PYRAMID BENCH

This loop trip includes Pyramid Lake Drive and the eastern part of the Pyramid Lake trail.

PYRAMID LAKE DRIVE rises steadily for 6.7 km to where it is gated at Pyramid Lake. It is an easy cycling ascent, mostly on pavement and offers a fine view of colourful Pyramid Mountain that dominates the skyline north of Jasper and reflects its image in Pyramid Lake.

The PYRAMID BENCH trail is marked by "#2" signs. It is a wide hiking and horse trail with roots and rocks exposed and therefore, best ridden in the downhill mode. A maze of trails crosses this area. However, the "bench" route is easy to find - simply stay left at all the junctions.

The trail meanders through some of the best groves of Douglas fir that you'll ever find. The bench is a river terrace created by the Athabasca River eroding a channel through thick deposits of glacial debris. Lake Edith, Lake Annette and the Jasper Park Lodge can be spotted from the bench. Hoodoos have been eroded into the side of the river terrace.

If you are feeling lazy, you could have a friend drive you to the top of the road and pick you up at the bottom of the hill an hour later - that way you are spared the effort of cycling up the hill before you enjoy the downhill ride.

RATING
Tough
DISTANCE
15.0 km round trip
TIME
3 - 4 hours round trip
ELEVATION GAIN
140 m (460 ft)
MAP
83 D/16 Jasper

ACCESS
The community center at the corner of Pyramid Avenue and Pyramid Lake Drive in Jasper makes a good place to start this loop trip.

7 Map 8
TRAIL NUMBER SEVEN
(MALIGNE CANYON TO OLD FORT POINT)

This loop trip includes trail number seven, Maligne Lake Road and the Jasper Park Lodge access road. This is not a remote wilderness ride - you might call it the Jasper golf course tour. It does offer access to many interesting features of the urbanized mountain environment and the opportunity to spend a lazy afternoon if you are tired of riding more macho cliff-hanging trails. You might even consider stopping for a spot of tea at the Jasper Park Lodge!

Ride along number seven trail, a bumpy, sandy horse trail along the river or take the paved road to Maligne Canyon which is one of the most popular attractions in Jasper. In its depths you can see where subterranean channels empty water which has flowed underground 16 km from Medicine Lake. Bicycles are not allowed on the Maligne Canyon interpretive trail but several bridges offer access to the canyon from the Maligne Lake Road. Avoid conflict with hikers along the canyon rim; park your bike and walk the trails along the river. The trail follows the canyon to the souvenir stand at the top where you can buy Michael Jackson day glow cycling gloves. They are only available for the left hand.

The trail back to Old Fort Point starts on the south side of the bridge on the Maligne River Road at the upper end of the canyon. It is a smooth, sandy horse trail, cushioned by pine needles and marked with "#7" signs. Watch for horses.

RATING
Tender
DISTANCE
23.1 km round trip
TIME
3 - 5 hours round trip
ELEVATION GAIN
120 m (400 ft)
MAPS
83 D/16 Jasper
83 C/13 Medicine Lake

ACCESS
Old Fort Point, on the east side of the Athabasca River near the south side of Jasper townsite makes a good trailhead for this trip.

8 Map 9
VALLEY OF FIVE LAKES
& WABASSO LAKE

This is a loop trip utilizing the Valley of Five Lakes trail and the Icefields Parkway (Hwy. 93).

The trail traverses a number of sandstone ridges that resemble the Canadian Shield in northern Ontario or Manitoba. When the trail runs parallel to the ridges, it is mostly smooth and sandy. When it crosses the ridges it is rough and rocky. Most of this trail provides good cycling on relatively level terrain. Watch for hikers since this is a popular trail.

RATING
Tough
DISTANCE
36.8 km round trip
TIME
4 - 7 hours
ELEVATION GAIN
260 m (850 ft)
MAPS
83 D/16 Jasper
83 C/13 Medicine Lake

ACCESS
The trail starts at the Wabasso Lake trailhead 16 km south of Jasper on the Icefields Parkway (Hwy. 93). A shorter trip can be made by starting at the Valley of Five Lakes trailhead 10.4 km south of Jasper.

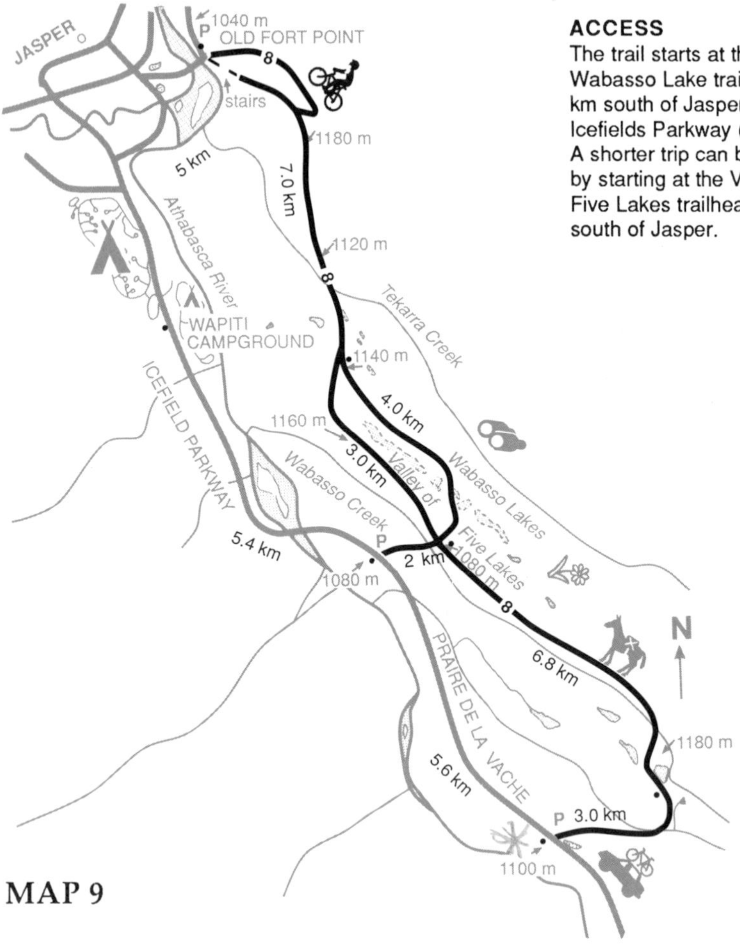

MAP 9

42

The south end of the trail is by far the roughest. After 3 km of traversing the ridges, the trail passes Wabasso Lake, a peaceful, weedy lake popular for fishing and a series of beaver ponds on Prairie de la Vache or Buffalo Prairie. About half-way to the Valley of Five Lakes the trail breaks out of the trees onto a dry open river terrace spotted with Douglas fir. Frost action and erosion along the terrace have exposed many boulders which have rolled down the bank and collected at the bottom of the slope and in the gullies.

The marsh along Wabasso Creek is a rich wildlife habitat. Great blue herons and beaver are among its inhabitants. The name Wabasso is derived from the Cree word for rabbit.

Follow the trail that crosses to the north side of the Valley of Five Lakes. A ring of jade green lines the bottom of each lake. Near Old Fort Point, the west branch of the trail ends with stairs while the east branch has a good gravel track leading down to the parking lot.

The return trip is a 16.4 km cycle along the Icefields Parkway.

Jo-Ann Draper in theValley of Five Lakes. There is a turquoise ring around the lake.

ay 90 - from * to Old Fort Point + then back along highway. Quite technical in spots. Easy in a day.

43

9 Map 10
WHIRLPOOL RIVER

The first 0.5 km of the Whirlpool Fire Road past the gate has been downgraded but most of it is a smooth gravel road that is partly vegetated.

Mount Edith Cavell rises to the north while Whirlpool Peak adorns the view on the south side of the fast and powerful Whirlpool River. At the 6.6 km point, the quiet waters of the pond at Whirlpool campground reflect the surrounding mountains and provides a strong contrast to the churning river nearby. The road ends at a wet meadow near some disused tool sheds and the remains of the Tie Camp Warden Cabin.

Past this point, the trail is a rough hiking trail quite unsuitable for cycling. The Tie Camp campground is 3.8 km further along the trail. At one time, trees were cut here and floated down the Whirlpool and Athabasca rivers to Jasper to be cut into railway ties.

RATING
Tender
DISTANCE
9.2 km
TIME
2 - 3 hours return
ELEVATION GAIN
30 m (100 ft)
MAPS
83 C/12 Athabasca Falls
83 D/9 Amethyst Lakes

ACCESS
Highway 93A branches off the Icefields Parkway. The Whirlpool Fire Road is located 15.5 km from the northern end of 93A and 9 km from the southern end of 93A at Athabasca Falls. Drive south on the Whirlpool Fire Road for 7 km to the parking lot and the gate. The right hand trail is a 0.5 km-long trail to Moab Lake while the left hand trail is the continuation of the Whirlpool Fire Road.

HIKING OPTION
ATHABASCA PASS
This historic trail continues for another 40 km to the Committee's Punchbowl on Athabasca Pass. David Thompson, one of Canada's greatest fur trade explorers, made the first recorded crossing of this pass in 1811. The pass became the main fur trading route through the Rockies for almost half a century.

Whirlpool Peak near the Whirlpool River Fire road.

MAP 10

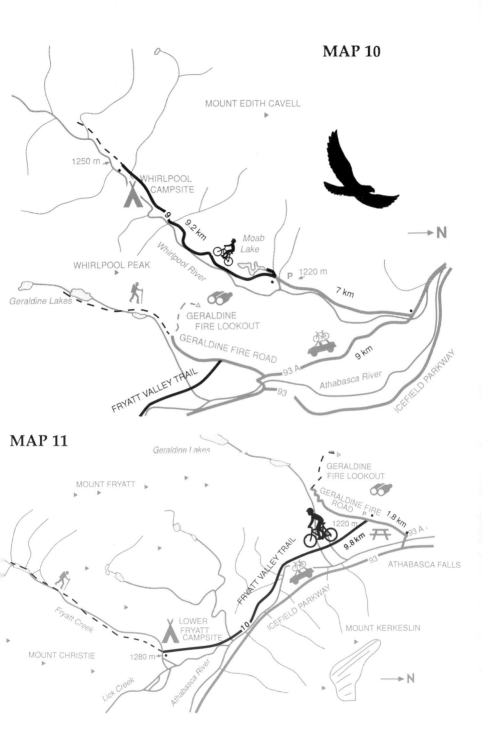

MOUNT EDITH CAVELL

1250 m

WHIRLPOOL
CAMPSITE

9

9.2 km

Moab
Lake

→N

WHIRLPOOL PEAK

Whirlpool River

P 1220 m

7 km

Geraldine Lakes

GERALDINE
FIRE LOOKOUT

GERALDINE FIRE ROAD

9 km

93 A

FRYATT VALLEY TRAIL

Athabasca River

93

ICEFIELD PARKWAY

MAP 11

Geraldine Lakes

GERALDINE
FIRE LOOKOUT

MOUNT FRYATT

GERALDINE FIRE
ROAD

P

1.8 km

1220 m

93 A

9.8 km

FRYATT VALLEY TRAIL

93

ATHABASCA FALLS

Fryatt Creek

LOWER
FRYATT
CAMPSITE

10

ICEFIELD PARKWAY

MOUNT KERKESLIN

MOUNT CHRISTIE

1280 m

Athabasca River

Lick Creek

→N

45

10 Map 11
FRYATT CREEK

Fryatt Lake mirrors the peaks surrounding a beautiful alpine valley. It is a popular hiking and climbing destination despite a long access road which makes hiking rather monotonous. By cycling the lower part of the trail, it possible to reach the upper Fryatt Valley on a long day trip. It is a pleasant cycling trip even if you venture no further than the Lower Fryatt campground.

The lower Fryatt Valley trail was once a road but it has not seen traffic for many years. Except for some short sections of narrow trail and rocky areas where cobbles protrude from the forest floor it offers mostly smooth cycling on a carpet of pine needles as far as the campsite on Fryatt Creek at the 9.8 km point,

At 6 km the trail passes close to the Athabasca River at a small beach. The sound of cars on the highway across the river reminds you that you have not strayed far from the pavement. At 7.6 km the trail emerges briefly from the trees at the edge of Fryatt Creek where erosion of the bank has formed rudimentary hoodoos. Mount Christie and Brussels Peak are the dominant peaks in the Park Ranges to the west.

The lower Fryatt campground is situated on the banks of Fryatt Creek under the shadow of the pyramidal mass of Fryatt Peak.

RATING
Tough
DISTANCE
9.8 km to Lower Fryatt
Campground
TIME
3 - 4 hours round trip
ELEVATION GAIN
60 m (200 feet)
MAP
83 C/12 Athabasca Falls

ACCESS
The Geraldine Lake Fire
Road branches off Highway
93A, 1 km north of the
junction with the Icefields
Parkway at Athabasca Falls.
Follow the gravel Fire Road
for 1.8 km to the start of the
Fryatt Valley hiking trail.

HIKING OPTION
FRYATT LAKE
It is best to leave the bike
and hike if you continue past
the campsite since the trail
climbs steeply up the Fryatt
Valley from this point on. It
is another 7.2 km and 440 m
of elevation gain to Fryatt
Lake.

11 Map 12
ATHABASCA RIVER

This route follows an old road up the Athabasca River. The road, which is slightly vegetated and covered in pine needles is mostly smooth with occasional rough spots including a section of corduroy road. The trail loses elevation for the first 7 km to Big Bend campsite.

At Big Bend the trail breaks out of the pine forest and the traveller is rewarded with views of Dragon Peak, Fortress Mountain and Quincy Peak. At 13 km the trail forks. The west fork reaches a dead end at the Chaba Warden Cabin. The cabin overlooks a pond which is the richest shade of blue you'll find anywhere in the Rockies.

A suspension bridge built over the Athabasca River in 1985 marks the end of the road for cycling.

RATING
Tough
DISTANCE
16.5 km one way
TIME
4 - 5 hours return
ELEVATION GAIN
30 m (100 ft)
ELEVATION LOSS
60 m (200 ft)
MAPS
83 C/12 Athabasca Falls
83 C/5 Fortress Lake

ACCESS
The trail begins at Sunwapta Falls 55 km south of Jasper on the south side of the Icefields Parkway. Walk your bike across the bridge past all the noncyclists looking at Sunwapta Falls. Cycle the trail south toward Big Bend.

Daryl Ronsky and his well trained bicycle crossing the Athabasca River on the new suspension bridge.

47

This trail was the first backcountry bicycling route that we attempted. Jo-Ann and I were cycling from Jasper to Banff on touring bikes and were looking for a campsite. We bumped and dragged our ten speed bikes over the trail to Big Bend Campsite. The other campers looked a little surprised to see two cyclists so far from road, especially since mountain bikes had not yet been invented.

HIKING OPTION
FORTRESS LAKE
The trail beyond the suspension bridge has been recently rebuilt and offers hiking access to Fortress Lake. If you want to hike to Fortress Lake be prepared for a difficult ford of the Chaba River.

MAP 12

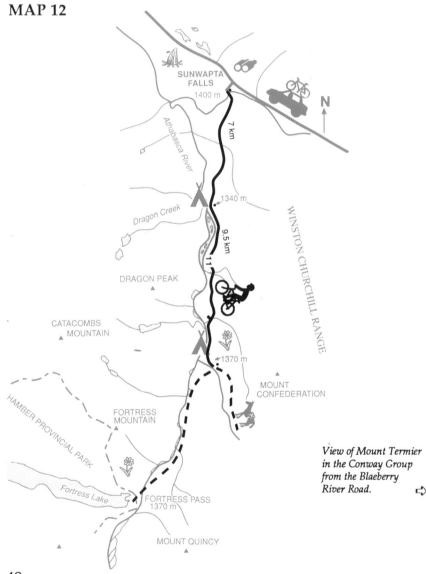

View of Mount Termier in the Conway Group from the Blaeberry River Road. ⇨

YOHO PARK

12 MAP 13
TALLY-HO ROAD

The Tally-Ho Road, a designated bicycle trail, is a 3.0 km stretch of road that was abandoned when the Trans-Canada Highway was upgraded. It connects the Trans-Canada Highway and the Emerald Lake Road. It is of little interest in itself but it could be useful as a diversion for someone riding between Field and Emerald Lake.

RATING
Tender
DISTANCE
3.0 km
ELEVATION GAIN
36 m (120 ft)
MAP
82 N/7 Golden

ACCESS
The trailhead is located at a picnic area on the west side of the Trans-Canada Highway, 1 km south of Field. A boulder barricade marks the start of the road.

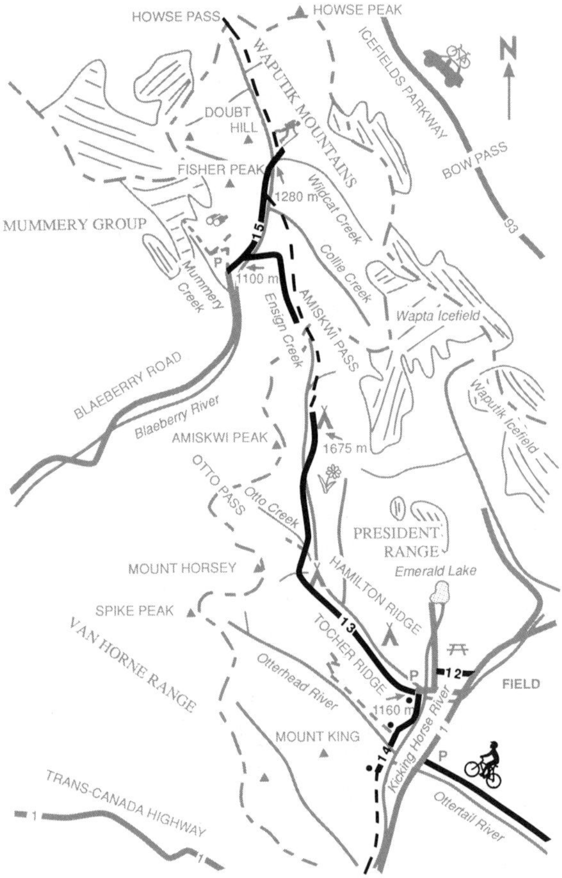

MAP 13

13 MAP 13
AMISKWI RIVER FIRE ROAD

The Amiskwi River Fire Road is a long smooth, gravel road that provides easy and very enjoyable cycling. It is designated for cycling as far as the Amiskwi III campsite.

Bridges in the Amiskwi Valley have a history of washing out in the spring so fording the river may be necessary.

Few people hike into this remote and beautiful valley because of the long distance to Amiskwi III campsite and Amiskwi Pass which can take several days there and back. A bicycle can be a great asset to the hiker. Although the pass can then be accessed in one long day, it is highly recommended that you reserve this trail for an overnight trip.

The route starts as a gravel road that climbs steadily for the first 2 km. The valley has been burnt from Fire Creek at 15 km almost all the way to Amiskwi Pass. The burn area is covered in a profusion of fireweed and other colourful wildflowers in midsummer.

At 17 km take the right fork and cross Otto Creek on a bridge. The road becomes increasingly rough and vegetated and at 22 km the road crosses the Amiskwi River on another bridge. Cycling is permitted as far as the Amiskwi III campsite at km 24.

The return trip is a very fast and enjoyable ride.

RATING
Tender
DISTANCE
24 km one way to Amiskwi III campsite
TIME
6 - 9 hours round trip
ELEVATION GAIN
520 m (1700 ft)
MAPS
82 N/10 Blaeberry River
82 N/7 Golden

ACCESS
Drive 2.6 km south from Field on the Trans-Canada Highway. Follow the Emerald Lake Road for 1.5 km to the Natural Bridge Turnoff. Drive past the Natural Bridge parking area, the Animal Salt Lick and Emerald Creek to the Amiskwi River bridge and picnic area. The Amiskwi Fire Road starts at the north end of the parking lot on the west side of the Amiskwi River.

HIKING OPTION
AMISKWI PASS
The road ends at about 29 km and a hiking trail continues to Amiskwi Falls at 32 km and Amiskwi Pass at 36 km.There is a private hut past the boundary of Yoho Park near Amiskwi Pass. For information call Shirley Green at (604) 343-6397 in Field British Columbia. The hut can also be reached via the Blaeberry Valley (#15).

51

14 MAP 13
KICKING HORSE FIRE ROAD

The first 7.8 km of the Kicking Horse Fire Road is a short, easy cycle paralleling the Kicking Horse River. The remainder of the trail to Porcupine Creek, which has been designated as a cycling trail, is a rough, overgrown seldom travelled trail that is of no interest for cycling.

The first 4.0 km offers remarkably level and smooth riding on dirt road covered with pine needles. The road forks at the Otterhead River - the Otterhead Fire Road to the right climbs up along the river. The Kicking Horse Fire Road to the left continues for 3.8 km, reaching a log bridge over the Otterhead River in 0.8 km. After crossing the bridge, the road becomes slightly rutted and alders and washouts are beginning the slow process of reclaiming the road. Several large Douglas fir create a change from the pine forest.

The road dead ends at an avalanche path and stream which have obliterated any trace of a road. To continue further means dragging your bike through devil's club, a nasty shrub covered in poisoned prickles that create intense itching. Welcome to B.C. bushwhacking.

RATING
Tender
DISTANCE
7.8 km one way
TIME
2 hours return
ELEVATION GAIN
30 m (100 ft)
MAP
82 N/7 Golden

ACCESS
Drive 2.6 km south from Field on the Trans-Canada Highway to the Emerald Lake Road. Follow it for 1.5 km to the Natural Bridge turnoff. Drive past the Natural Bridge parking area, the Animal Salt Lick and Emerald Creek to the Amiskwi River bridge and picnic area. The signed trailhead is located at the south side of the parking lot on the west side of the Amiskwi River.

Deb Ritchie. - A mountain goat of a cyclist on the Ottertail Fire Road.

BLAEBERRY RIVER ROAD

The Blaeberry Road changes regularly as floods, landslides and logging activity change the access. It is a wild remote valley that exhibits the power of nature on a grand scale. From Mummery Creek the Mummery Glacier can be seen dropping down from the Mummery Group.

Mummery Creek is a good starting place although you may prefer to cycle the entire road from the Trans-Canada Highway. From Mummery Creek don't take the obvious logging road which climbs up to the Mummery Glacier trail. The Blaeberry Road stays close to the river for 10 km to Wildcat Creek. Except for the occasional washout it is a smooth gravel road providing easy cycling

Huge avalanche paths several kilometres wide have cleared swaths down the slopes of Fisher Peak to the west. Cutblocks, burns and gravel flats create variety in the types of vegetation. At Doubt Hill, the towers of Mount Termier can be seen in the Conway Group. The Freshfield Icefield lies out of sight to the west.

At the bridge by Doubt Hill, a sign indicates the start of a 14 km hiking trail to Howse Pass below Howse Peak which raises its glacier shrouded peak to the north. The road fades away into the last cutblock at Wildcat Creek.

It is an easy downhill ride back to Mummery Creek.

RATING
Tender
DISTANCE
10 km
TIME
2 - 3 hours round trip
ELEVATION GAIN
180 m (600 ft)
MAP
82 N/10 Blaeberry River

ACCESS
Drive 17 km west of Golden on the Trans-Canada Highway to the Blaeberry Road which is 400 m west of the bridge over the Blaeberry River. Follow this gravel road up the Blaeberry River for 40 km to the Mummery Creek Recreation Site.

HIKING / CYCLING OPTION
ENSIGN CREEK
A logging road has been built up Ensign Creek to within 1 km of Amiskwi Pass. There is a private hut on the pass. For information call Shirley Green in Field, British Columbia at (604) 343-6397.

16 MAP 14
OTTERTAIL RIVER FIRE ROAD

The Ottertail Fire Road follows the north side of the Ottertail River to McArthur Creek Warden cabin. It is mostly a smooth, well-graded gravel road with some steep sections and several washed out culverts that can deceive the unattentive cyclist.

This valley has a very different character from the Ice River, one valley to the south. The Ottertail has a dry, open lodgepole pine forest typical of the east slopes of the Rockies whereas the Ice River has a fir and cedar forest typical of British Columbia. The steep faces of the Ottertail Range rise to the south.

There is a backcountry campground at McArthur Creek. At the McArthur Warden Cabin, the trail breaks into the open to offer an inspiring view of the north face of Mount Goodsir. If there were a phone booth in this beautiful valley, you might be tempted to phone in sick on Monday morning.

RATING
Tender
DISTANCE
14.5 to McArthur Creek
Warden Cabin
TIME
3 - 4 hours round trip
ELEVATION GAIN
305 m (1000 feet)
MAPS
82 N/7 Golden
82 N/8 Lake Louise

ACCESS
The Ottertail Fire Road begins 8.5 km south-west of Field on the east side of the Trans-Canada Highway and north of the bridge over the Ottertail River.

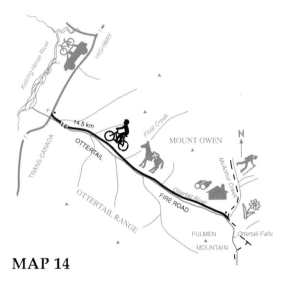

MAP 14

HIKING OPTIONS
OTTERTAIL FALLS
 A 2 km trail leads up river from the Warden Cabin to Ottertail Falls where the Ottertail River spills into a canyon. This trail continues up the valley, goes over OTTERTAIL PASS and descends Ochre Creek to the Ochre Bed on the Banff-Windermere Parkway.
The GOODSIR PASS trail branches off the Ottertail Pass trail near Ottertail Falls. It takes a more southerly route into Kootenay National Park.
The MCARTHUR CREEK trail travels north over McArthur Pass to the Lake O'Hara area.

17 MAP 15
ICE RIVER FIRE ROAD – CROZIER LOOP

This long loop trip includes the Ice River Fire Road in Yoho National Park and the Crozier Road along the Beaverfoot River. The 16 km ride to the Lower Ice River Warden Cabin is an easy day trip. The complete circuit can be ridden as a long day trip or as an overnight trip.

Double track on the Ice River Fire road.
Gord and Deb Ritchie

RATING
Tender
DISTANCE
66 km round trip
TIME
8 - 13 hours
ELEVATION GAIN
300 m (1000 ft)
MAPS
82 N/2 McMurdo
82 N/1 Mount Goodsir

ACCESS
Hoodoo Creek Campground is located 22 km south-west of Field on the Trans-Canada Highway. The south fork of the campground road leads to Deerlodge trail. The Ice River Fire Road begins at the gate at the south end of the parking area.

CAMPING
Parks Canada has not provided a backcountry campsite on the Ice River. The best camping is near the bridge over the Beaverfoot River outside of Yoho Park. Beaverfoot Lodge on the Crozier Road offers overnight accommodation and a source of "suds" for thirsty cyclists.

The ICE RIVER FIRE ROAD provides easy cycling on a smooth, well-graded road. The road is vegetated in places, but the park wardens drive it occasionally and thus keep it smooth for cycling. Large spruce, cedar and fir make up the forest and devil's club, the bane of the mountaineer, grows as understory. This typical interior British Columbia forest has a much different character from the lodgepole pine forest found on the other side of the Continental Divide.

When you cross the Ice River, you are leaving Yoho National park and entering Crown Land that is managed for timber production. The difference serves as a clear reminder of what National Parks are for.

The CROZIER ROAD, also known as the BEAVERFOOT ROAD, is a well-kept gravel road which services the logging in the area. On weekends you won't likely have to compete with logging trucks. The Crozier Road passes a picnic area north of Beaverfoot Lodge with a view of Wapta Falls.

Getting to the Crozier Road from the Lower Ice River Warden Cabin is a little more challenging. Cross the Ice River on a good foot bridge and push or carry your bike out of the stream valley up a steep trail which soon levels out. Once you get to the top of the river terrace, cross the clearing to the rough road through the cutblocks. The route steadily improves to become a gravel logging road. The bridge over the Beaverfoot River to the Crozier Road is in good condition.

HIKING OPTION
UPPER ICE RIVER
The hiking trail up the Upper Ice River leads to a remote and wild valley that usually contains more grizzly bears than people. A large igneous intrusion has eroded to form the North and South Towers of Mount Goodsir. The area is of interest to both geologists and climbers.

Gerhardt Lepp Riding through ⇨
cutblock north of the Beaverfoot Road.
Vermilion Range in the background.

KOOTENAY PARK

18 MAP 15
CROZIER ROAD
(KOOTENAY CROSSING TO
KICKING HORSE RIVER)

This long but easy fat-tire trip follows the West
Kootenay Fire Road, logging roads and the Crozier
Road up the Kootenay River to its headwaters, then
descends the Beaverfoot River to the Trans-Canada
Highway. It could be cycled as part of a multi-day
tour or a shuttle could be arranged at one of the
trailheads. It is 172 km by highway from Kootenay
Crossing to the Crozier Road via Radium and
Golden, a long drive for a shuttle. The first 44.6 km
of the Crozier Road to the Paul Creek B.C. Forest
Service Recreation Site is open to traffic and suitable
for a small car.

WEST KOOTENAY FIRE ROAD - From Kootenay
Crossing cycle up the hill within sight of the Warden
Station. This is the steepest hill on the entire route.
After 1 km take the right fork. The next 9 km to the
park boundary is a gravel and packed dirt road
winding through pine, spruce, fir and willows.
Numerous saplings have been stripped by elk rub-
bing their antlers. At 9.8 km take the left fork - the
right fork goes 1 km to a bridge crossing the Kote-
nay River and joins the hiking trail up the east side of
the Kootenay.

Past the park boundary you may notice five foot-
long poles leaning against trees and boxes nailed to
the trees above the poles. These are "sets" used by a
trapper. Bait is placed in the box at the top of the pole
and a snare or trap is positioned to catch an inquisi-
tive marten running up the pole.

The 11.9 km of road from the Kootenay Park
boundary to Paul Creek is the roughest part of the
trip. Willows and alders encroach on the road which
is rutted and heavily vegetated in places. There are
several creeks to cross. The road improves after
reaching a cutblock where a view to the Vermilion
Range opens up. After crossing a bridge over the
upper Kootenay River, the road joins the wide,
smooth, gravel Crozier Road near the Paul Creek
Recreation Site.

RATING
Tender
DISTANCE
66.5 km one way
TIME
5 - 8 hours one way
ELEVATION GAIN
126 m (415 ft)
ELEVATION LOSS
305 m (1000 ft)
MAPS
82 K/16 Spillimacheen
82 N/1 Mount Goodsir
82 N/2 McMurdo

SOUTH-EAST ACCESS
Park at the Kootenay
Crossing Warden Station on
the west side of the Banff-
Windermere Highway (Hwy.
93), 51 km south of the
Banff-Kootenay boundary at
Vermilion Pass and 42 km
north of the Kootenay Park
west gate at Radium. The
trail starts on the south side
of the complex at a gated
road about 200 m past a
house.

NORTH-WEST ACCESS
The Crozier Road, also
known as the Beaverfoot
Road, joins the Trans-
Canada Highway 1 km west
of the Yoho Park west gate,
30.5 km west of Field and 26
km east of Golden. The
bridge over the Kicking
Horse River, 1 km south on
the Crozier Road is a good
rendezvous spot.

The CROZIER ROAD provides 44.6 km of fast, easy cycling to the Kicking Horse River and the Trans-Canada Highway. The yellow signs indicate the distance in kilometres to Golden. Cutblocks alternate with mature mixed forest. Near the highway, Beaverfoot Lodge provides a refreshment stop and a base for side trips which could keep you busy for several days.

HIKING / CYCLING OPTIONS
Dainard Lake
Ice River (#17)
Wapta Falls
Wolverine Pass
Moose Creek
Hatch Creek

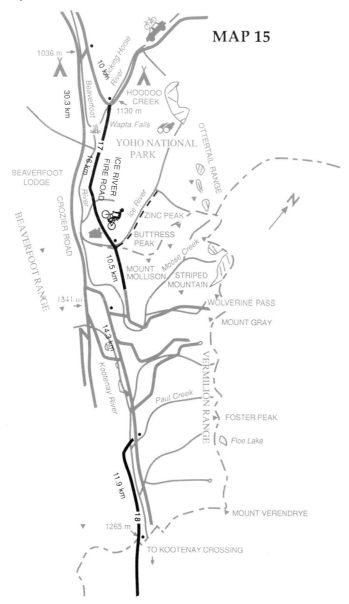

MAP 15

19 MAP 16
WEST KOOTENAY FIRE ROAD

The Dolly Varden section of the West Kootenay Fire Road connects the Kootenay Crossing Warden Station to Crook's Meadow group camp. The wide paved shoulders of Highway 93 can be used for the return trip.

The fire road, a smooth, dirt track winding through mature pine, spruce, poplar and Douglas fir forest, offers a pleasant but unspectacular ride. All streams are bridged. The steep rocky climb at the start is the only hill on the trip. The northern section of the Kootenay Fire Road (#18), branches to the north 1 km from Kootenay Crossing and parallels the Kootenay River for 9 km to the park boundary. Tangle Peak dominates the view from the south end.

RATING
Tender
DISTANCE
20.6 km round trip
TIME
2 hours round trip
ELEVATION GAIN
30 m (100 ft)
MAP
82 K/16 Spillimacheen

NORTH ACCESS
Park at the Kootenay Crossing Warden Station on the west side of the Banff-Windermere Highway (Hwy. 93), 51 km south of the Banff-Kootenay boundary at Vermilion Pass and 42 km north of the Kootenay Park west gate at Radium. The trail starts from the south side of the complex at a gated road about 200 m past a staff house.

SOUTH ACCESS
Crook's Meadow group campground 9.1 km south of Kootenay Crossing on the west side of the Banff-Windermere Highway (Hwy. 93). The gate on the group camp is usually locked. Cycle to the west side of the campground and look for a gated road at the edge of the trees.

Trolls take their toll at Dolly Varden Creek on the West Kootenay Fire Road. Colynn Kerr

CYCLING OPTION
The West Kootenay Fire Road can be combined with the East Kootenay Fire Road (#20) for a longer loop of 42.7 km.

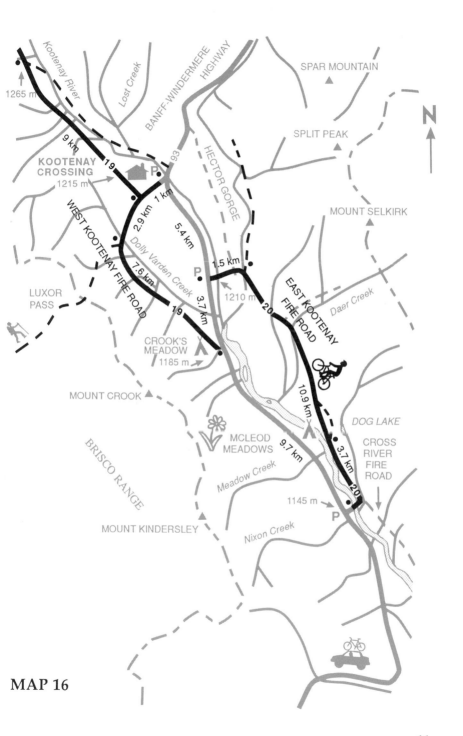

KOOTENAY RIVER

Kootenay River

Lost Creek

BANFF-WINDERMERE HIGHWAY

SPAR MOUNTAIN

1265 m

9 km

19

KOOTENAY
CROSSING

1215 m

P

93

2.9 km

1 km

SPLIT PEAK

HECTOR GORGE

5.4 km

MOUNT SELKIRK

WEST KOOTENAY FIRE ROAD

7.6 km

Dolly Varden Creek

1.5 km

P

1210 m

20

EAST KOOTENAY FIRE ROAD

Daer Creek

LUXOR
PASS

19

3.7 km

CROOK'S
MEADOW

1185 m

10.9 km

MOUNT CROOK

DOG LAKE

BRISCO RANGE

MCLEOD
MEADOWS

9.7 km

3.7 km

CROSS
RIVER
FIRE
ROAD

Meadow Creek

1145 m

20

MOUNT KINDERSLEY

Nixon Creek

P

MAP 16

61

20 MAP 16
EAST KOOTENAY FIRE ROAD

The East Kootenay Fire Road is a pleasant, easy cycle on the east side of the Kootenay River from the south access bridge to the confluence of the Kootenay and Vermilion rivers. It is a good trip in either direction. All river and creek crossings are bridged and you can expect a smooth gravel road most of the way.

The southern part of the trail stays close to the river with its broad alluvial flats. Mount Kindersley and Mount Crook in the Brisco Range form the western side of the valley. The northern part is a pleasant but unspectacular valley bottom road winding through pine forest. Large Douglas firs stand among the smaller and younger pine trees. Fire scars in the thick bark of the firs attest to the fact that these trees survived the fire that swept the valley in 1926. The thin barked pines did not survive, but took advantage of the excellent seed bed and growing conditions after the fire to produce the next generation.

The broad paved shoulders of Highway 93 provide a 13.4 km return trip to the trailhead.

RATING
Tender
DISTANCE
29.5 km round trip
TIME
2 - 3 hours round trip
ELEVATION GAIN
65 m (200 ft)
MAPS
82 K/16 Spillimacheen
82 J/13 Mount Assiniboine
82 J/12 Tangle Peak

SOUTH ACCESS
The trailhead is located at a bridge over the Kootenay River on the east side of the Banff-Windermere Highway (Hwy. 93), 0.6 km north of Nixon Creek and 18.8 km south of Kootenay Crossing.

NORTH ACCESS
The northern trailhead is a nondescript gated unmarked road on the west side of Highway 93, 5.4 km south of Kootenay Crossing.

CYCLING OPTION
The East and West Kootenay fire roads could be combined in a 42.7 km loop trip.

Mike Sainas at Egypt Lake. ⇨
Ball Range in the background.

BANFF
PARK

21 MAP 17
SKOKI VALLEY

Fat-tired backcountry travel will allow you to get into Skoki Valley on a day trip, rather than an overnight backpacking trip. It is the only designated bicycle trail in Banff Park that passes through alpine meadows. The trail climbs over two alpine passes, Boulder Pass and Deception Pass and then descends through one of the most beautiful vallys in the Rockies to a small lodge. Save this trip for dry weather since the trail can get quite muddy. Because of the elevation gain, it is a long day trip, even for a bicycle. Get an early start and go prepared for sudden violent storms - the Skoki Valley is famous for them. We cycled this trail in August after a two week spell of scorchingly hot weather. We got a late start and were further delayed by a hike to Red Deer Lakes. Clouds filled the valley, the rain turned to snow and then it got dark. With a pair of spare socks for mitts I could

RATING
Terrific - dry weather only
DISTANCE
14.8 km to Skoki Lodge
TIME
7 - 9 hours return
ELEVATION GAIN
770 m (2520 ft)
MAPS
82 N/8 Lake Louise
 82 N/9 Hector Lake

ACCESS
From Lake Louise townsite, follow the access road toward Lake Louise Ski Area. Two kilometres north-east of the Trans-Canada Highway, turn right onto the gravel road which leads to the Fish Creek trailhead parking lot . The trail to Skoki continues up the Temple Lodge road or ski-out past the locked gate.

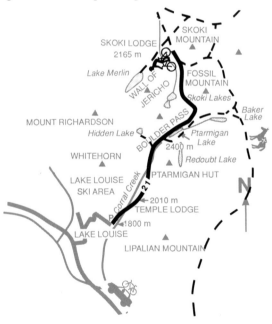

MAP 17

barely hang on to the brakes as I bumped down the trail through the mud to the car. I hope your trip is less eventful.

The first 3.5 km is steep cycling up a smooth gravel road to Temple Chalet, part of the Lake Louise Ski Area. The gravel road fades into a wide dirt trail through subalpine forest with a carpet of grouseberries on the forest floor. An avalanche slope provides a break in the forest and a view of Mount Temple and the Horseshoe Glacier at the head of the Paradise Valley.

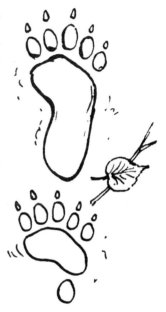

Cycle through the subalpine meadows along Corral Creek. The trail is in good condition considering the high volume of horse traffic. Ptarmigan Hut, also known as Halfway Hut, is a log cabin that provides shelter for skiers, hikers or cyclists travelling to Skoki Lodge. The hut is for day use only. The trail climbs steeply for the next kilometre to Ptarmigan Lake on Boulder Pass. As you push your bike up the hill, listen for the marmots and pikas that find shelter in the jumble of rocks along the trail.

North of Ptarmigan Lake the trail levels out for about 1 km but you must again push your fat tires up the treeless alpine slopes leading to Deception Pass. A patch of snow usually survives through the summer at the summit of the pass. The pass offers a panoramic view of several alpine valleys, Redoubt Mountain and the glacier capped peaks near Lake Louise.

The next 3.6 km is a 310 m descent to Skoki Lodge. The trail is rutted but rideable. Watch for horses that may be hidden from view by clumps of subalpine fir and larches. The best mountain scenery has been saved for last - the Skoki Lakes, framed by Ptarmigan Peak, Pika Peak and the Wall of Jericho. The trail drops back into the trees and soon arrives at Skoki Lodge where you would be wise to enquire about afternoon tea and learn more about the history of one Canada's first ski resorts. Reservations for lodging can be make through Lake Louise Ski Area. There is a backcountry campsite a further 1.2 km down the trail.

22 MAP 18
REDEARTH CREEK TO EGYPT LAKE

This designated cycling route follows Redearth Creek Fire Road and the Pharaoh Creek trail to Egypt Lake. All trails are signed and creeks are bridged. Cycling provides same day access to numerous short hikes in this beautiful subalpine valley such as Talc Lake, Mummy Lake, Scarab Lake, Haiduk Lake and Sphinx Lake. Pharaoh Peaks were named because of their resemblance to a row of Egyptian mummies.

The first 10.8 km to Redearth Creek Warden Cabin is smooth gravel road. Begin by grinding up the Redearth Creek Fire Road for 7.2 km to the bridge and campground. The remaining 3.6 km to the cabin is less steep.

Pharaoh Creek trail is a more challenging single track which is sometimes rocky and sometimes smooth. It climbs gently but steadily through an open subalpine valley with willows and clumps of spruce and fir. At the lower end of the trail there is a short steep section where shale slabs rise above the creek. Higher up, the trail crosses the creek numerous times on small log bridges.

Egypt Lake is a beautiful subalpine lake with a public shelter and campground nearby. Several interesting hiking trails fan out from the lake.

It is an easy and enjoyable return ride. Although not frequented by horse riders, this trail is a very popular hiking route. Be sure not to spoil a hikers enjoyment.

July '90 - technical @ beginning, then follows fire road to *, from there, good bike signs, so can't get into Pharaoh Shadow Lake or Egypt easy. 3-4 hours.

RATING
Tough
DISTANCE
19.8 km to Egypt Lake
14.3 km to Shadow Lake
TIME
5 - 8 hours return trip
ELEVATION GAIN
610 m (2000 ft)
MAP
82 O/4 Banff

ACCESS
From Banff, drive west on the Trans-Canada Highway for 20 km to the Redearth Creek trailhead. It is 10.5 km east of Castle Junction. The trail climbs the hill on the east end of the parking lot and joins the fire road 300 m further on.

CYCLING OPTION
SHADOW LAKE
This hiking trail departs from Redearth Creek Fire Road at the 10.8 km point and has been designated a bicycle route as far as Shadow Lake. The start of it does not look promising as a bicycle trail because it is rough and narrow leaving you no choice but to walk the bike. However, it soon improves as it enters more open and mature pine, fir and spruce forest where the trail is wide enough to cycle and the roots are small enough to ride over. Shadow Lake is an impressive lake with sheer cliffs and hanging glaciers of Mount Ball as a backdrop. Cycling can give you a head start for fishing the lake or hiking to Gibbon Pass, Ball Pass or Haiduk Lake.

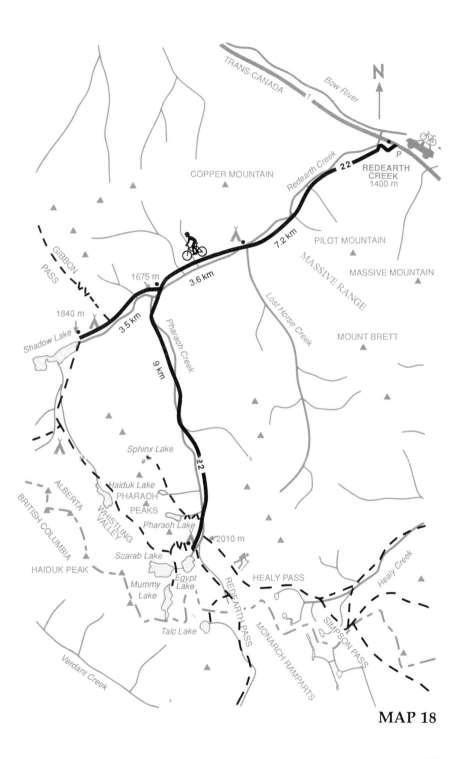

TRANS-CANADA

Bow River

1

N

COPPER MOUNTAIN

Redearth Creek

2.2

REDEARTH
CREEK
1400 m

P

PILOT MOUNTAIN

7.2 km

MASSIVE MOUNTAIN

GIBBON PASS

1675 m

3.6 km

MASSIVE RANGE

1840 m

3.5 km

Shadow Lake

Pharaoh Creek

Lost Horse Creek

MOUNT BRETT

9 km

Sphinx Lake

2.2

ALBERTA

Haiduk Lake

PHARAOH
PEAKS

BRITISH COLUMBIA

WHISTLING
VALLEY

Pharaoh Lake

HAIDUK PEAK

Scarab Lake

2010 m

HEALY PASS

Healy Creek

Mummy
Lake

Egypt
Lake

REDEARTH PASS

SIMPSON PASS

Talc Lake

MONARCH RAMPARTS

Verdant Creek

MAP 18

23 MAP 19
YA HA TINDA
TO SCOTCH CAMP

This route follows a road along the north shore of the Red Deer River from the Banff Park boundary to Scotch Camp. Cycling is permitted only as far as Scotch Camp even though the road runs for 70 km through the Front Ranges of Banff Park to Lake Minnewanka. Cycling this route is a good excuse to visit Ya Ha Tinda Ranch, a federal government ranch which supplies horses for backcountry patrols in the National Parks. The extensive meadows around the ranch turn a golden brown in late summer. The primitive public campsite on the ranch is popular with horseback riders.

The route to Scotch Camp is easy cycling on a level, high-grade gravel road with all creeks bridged. At 11.3 km there is a large steel bridge across a canyon in the Red Deer River and a pleasant campsite in meadows and open pine forest. South of the camp, the road is blocked and downgraded. A side road to a warden cabin runs through some of the most beautiful valley bottom meadows in Banff Park. The meadows are rich with the smell of sage and a wall of unnamed peaks beckons to the west.

RATING
Tender
DISTANCE
11.3 km
TIME
2 - 3 hours round trip
ELEVATION GAIN
105 m (350 ft)
MAP
82 O/12 Barrier Mountain

ACCESS
From Cochrane, drive 13 km west to the Forestry Trunk Road (S.R. 940). Drive 82 km north on this gravel road to Mountainaire Lodge at the Red Deer River. The lodge can also be reached by driving the road along the Red Deer River from Sundre. From the north side of the bridge, a road continues west for 37 km to the Banff Park boundary. When crossing the he Ya Ha Tinda Ranch, be sure to close any gates behind you.

MAP 19

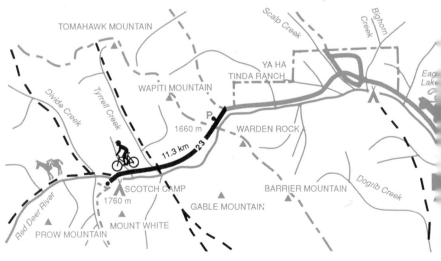

LAKE MINNEWANKA

The hiking trail along the north shore of Lake Minnewanka and past Ghost Lakes to the park boundary has been designated as a bicycle trail. The entire trail is a narrow, rolling, single track with very little elevation gain. The riding can be hard work but it is technical and fun. It would be reasonable to ride to the end of Lake Minnewanka and back in one day but not to the park boundary and back. The trail past Ghost Lakes, east of Lake Minnewanka, is very rough and rolling and past the limits of enjoyment for most cyclists. It may be worth persevering through this section if you can arrange a car shuttle at the Ghost River east of Devil's Gap. A more expensive option is to catch a ride on the ferry to the end of the lake and ride back to the dam.

Cycle past the locked gate, the boat launch and the picnic area to the trailhead. The trail starts as a wide paved path giving hikers access to Stewart Canyon and an excellent view across the lake. Past the junction with Stewart Canyon trail at the 2.0 km point, the trail climbs a hill through mature spruce forest with a deep moss carpet. This is the only hill of any significance on the route. The trail then crosses a scree slope, descends almost to lake level and follows the entire lake usually within sight of the shore. It offers continual variety: a stand of large Douglas firs, pleasant pebble beaches scattered with driftwood, pine forest with buffalo berry and a large spring gushing out of a rock face. The stream from Aylmer Canyon has built up a rocky outwash that will force you to walk the bike. Mounts Inglismaldie, Girouard and Peechee of the Fairholme Range rise to the south across the lake.

The east end of the trail is a rough, rocky banana masher of a trail that most people would not enjoy. Stay right at most junctions through a maze of roads and dirt bike trails which have a nasty habit of dead ending in the creek. Cross the gravel flats on a low gravel weir, turn north and push up the hill to the Ghost River road parking.

RATING
Tough
DISTANCE
23.4 km to east end of Lake Minnewanka
30.5 km to park boundary at Devil's Gap
TIME
5 - 8 hours round trip
ELEVATION GAIN
90 m (300 ft)
MAPS
82 O/6 Lake Minnewanka
82 O/3 Canmore

ACCESS
From Banff's east interchange on the Trans-Canada Highway , drive 6 km north on the Lake Minnewanka Road to the parking lot on the north side of the Minnewanka Dam. The actual trail starts east of the picnic and boat launching area.

DEVIL'S GAP ACCESS
From Cochrane, drive 13.0 km east on Highway 1A to the Forestry Trunk Road (S.R. 940). Drive north for 24.5 km on paved road to the Ghost River road, an unmarked, gated, gravel road 200 m north of Richard's Road. Please close the gate behind you. Drive 16.6 km west on the rough and bumpy Ghost River road and park at the top of a steep hill overlooking the Ghost River and Devil's Gap.

25 MAP 20
JOHNSON LAKE LOOP TRAILS

The Johnson Lake Loops are a series of ski trails that follow old roads around Johnson Lake and the powerline south of the lake. There is no particular destination, but it is a good place to ride for exercise and to let off some steam. The trails are marked with numbers nailed to trees. Johnson Lake is an odd creation formed by small earthen dams at both ends when the main dam on the west end broke in 1985 and lowered the level of the lake about one metre.

TRAIL #1 is a combination of road and trail winding through open pine forest. There is little elevation gain.

TRAIL #4 is a dirt road following the edge of the river terrace overlooking the Trans-Canada Highway and the Cascade River. Douglas firs grace the view of the valley and hoodoos protrude from the eroding edge of the terrace. Hoodoos are pillars of consolidated sand, gravel and rock. The surrounding sediments, which are not cemented together as firmly, erode away leaving pillars of the harder material.

RATING
Tender and Tough
DISTANCE
11.7 km
MAP
82 O/3 Canmore

ACCESS
From Banff's east interchange, drive north on the Lake Minnewanka Road. Take the first two major right turns and follow the signs to Johnson Lake.

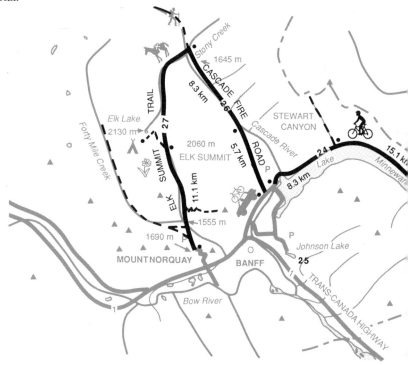

CASCADE FIRE ROAD

This cycling trip follows part of the Cascade Fire Road which extends for 70 km through the Front Ranges of Banff Park to Ya Ha Tinda Ranch on the Red Deer River. The area is known for its high grizzly population which has been studied in depth by Steve Herrero and his research team at the University of Calgary. Consequently the trail has been designated for cycling only as far as Stony Creek in order to reduce the chance of conflict with grizzlies.

The entire road to Stony Creek has a high-grade gravel surface. It travels between Cascade Mountain and the Palliser Range in a wide forested valley of mature pine with some willows and poplars. Meadows on the slopes high above the road make it a good place for spotting grazing elk and sheep.

RATING
Tender
DISTANCE
14.0 km one way
TIME
3 - 4 hours round trip
ELEVATION GAIN
210 m (700 ft)
MAPS
82 O/4 Banff
82 O/5 Castle Mountain

ACCESS
The Cascade Fire Road is a gated, unmarked gravel road on the north side of the Lake Minnewanka Road, 5 km north of Banff's east interchange. Its exact position is 1.3 km south of the dam on Lake Minnewanka and 800 m north of the Upper Bankhead Picnic Area which is the official trailhead and parking area.

HIKING OPTIONS
Cycling this road can give you a head start for hikes to Dormer Pass, Wigmore Creek or Flint's Park. The designated cycling route on the north side of Elk Summit (#27) is not recommended due to severe trail damage by commercial horse traffic.

MAP 20

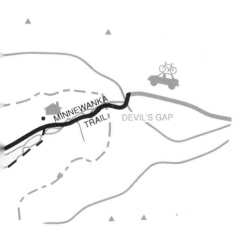

71

27 MAP 20
ELK SUMMIT

The Elk Summit trail follows the north fork of Forty Mile Creek to a pass between Cascade Mountain and Brewster Mountain. Most of the trail is wide, smooth, clearly signed and easy to follow.

From the Norquay parking lot the route follows a road across the lower ski runs of the ski area and a distinct avalanche chute. A smooth trail provides a downhill ride through solid pine and spruce forest to Forty Mile Creek bridge at the 3 km point.

The pungent smell of horse urine lingers in the deep, mossy forest past Forty Mile Creek, yet the trail is surprisingly smooth despite the heavy horse traffic. Push and peddle uphill along the forest bound trail. Near Elk Summit the forest opens up and becomes more alpine with subalpine fir, grouseberries and meadows along the creek. There is a view of Sulphur Mountain and Mount Norquay back down the valley.

In the summit meadows the trail becomes rutted, but still rideable. A 2 km hiking trail branches to the west through fir and larch forest to Elk Lake, an alpine tarn backed by the rugged limestone walls of Mount Brewster, a long thrust faulted ridge carved with glacial cirques.

The return trip to Forty Mile Creek is an easy downhill ride. Please watch carefully for horses and hikers.

RATING
Tough - dry weather only
DISTANCE
11.5 km
TIME
3 - 5 hours round trip
ELEVATION GAIN
505 m (1655 ft)
MAPS
82 O/4 Banff
82 O/5 Castle Mountain

ACCESS
From the west Banff interchange on the Trans-Canada Highway drive north up the long switchbacks of the Mount Norquay ski area access road. The trailhead lies at the far end of P3 parking lot.

CYCLING OPTION
ELK SUMMIT TO STONY CREEK
The trail down the north side of Elk Summit to Stony Creek on the Cascade River is a designated cycling trail. However, I do not recommend it for any but the most masochistic riders. Heavy commercial horse traffic has pounded poorly-drained organic soils into deep corrugations that are completely unrideable for a cyclist. The trail was rebuilt in the summer of 1986 but within two weeks of being smoothed out by the trail crew, horse traffic had again damaged the trail so badly it was unfit for cycling. If you persevere through the 9 km to Stony Creek you can ride out via the Cascade Fire Road (#26).

The trail on the north side of Elk Summit has been badly eroded and corrugated by horses.

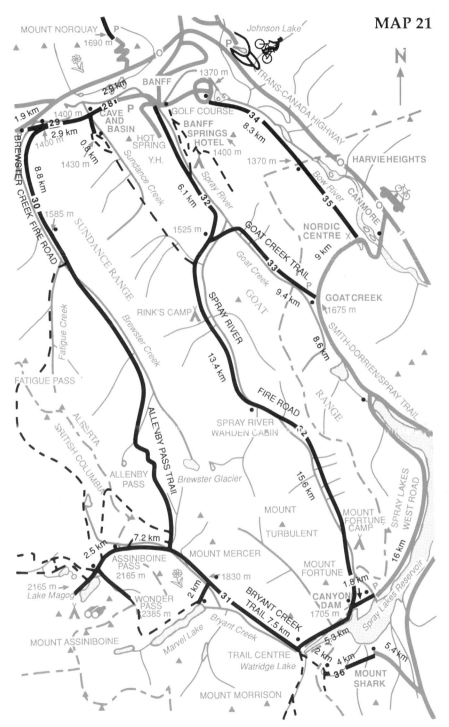

MAP 21

MOUNT NORQUAY
1690 m

Johnson Lake

TRANS-CANADA HIGHWAY

1370 m

2.9 km

BANFF

28

GOLF COURSE

34

8.3 km

HARVIE HEIGHTS

1.9 km

1400 m

29

CAVE
AND
BASIN

BANFF
SPRINGS
HOTEL

1400 m

CANMORE

2.9 km

0.8 km

1400 m

HOT
SPRING

Y.H.

1370 m

35

1430 m

Sundance Creek

Spray River

6.1 km

32

NORDIC
CENTRE

BREWSTER CREEK FIRE ROAD

8.8 km

30

1585 m

SUNDANCE RANGE

1525 m

GOAT CREEK TRAIL

33

9 km

9.4 km

GOAT CREEK
1675 m

Goat Creek

GOAT

Fatigue Creek

Brewster Creek

RINK'S CAMP

SPRAY RIVER

8.6 km

SMITH-DORRIEN/SPRAY TRAIL

FATIGUE PASS

13.4 km

RANGE

ALBERTA

BRITISH COLUMBIA

ALLENBY PASS TRAIL

FIRE ROAD

32

SPRAY RIVER
WARDEN CABIN

ALLENBY
PASS

Brewster Glacier

15.6 km

SPRAY LAKES WEST ROAD

MOUNT
TURBULENT

MOUNT
FORTUNE
CAMP

7.2 km

2.5 km

ASSINIBOINE
PASS
2165 m

MOUNT MERCER

1830 m

MOUNT
FORTUNE

16 km

2165 m
Lake Magog

2 km

31

WONDER
PASS
2385 m

1.8 km

Spray Lakes Reservoir

BRYANT CREEK
TRAIL 7.5 km

CANYON
DAM
1705 m

Marvel Lake

Bryant Creek

5.3 km

MOUNT ASSINIBOINE

TRAIL CENTRE
Watridge Lake

2 km

4 km

5.4 km

36

MOUNT
SHARK

MOUNT MORRISON

28 MAP 21
SUNDANCE TRAIL

The Sundance trail is a paved bicycle path alongside the Bow River and Sundance Creek. It provides access to Sundance Canyon trail, a rugged 2.4 km interpretive trail which winds through the sloping limestone slabs of the creek.

From the parking lot at Cave and Basin, cycle past the pool to a paved path leading up the Bow River. Mount Bourgeau and Mount Brett, the main peaks of the Massive Range, stand to the west. The Healy Creek road is a gated gravel road which joins the Sundance trail at the 2.9 km point. The paved path climbs through the pines to a picnic area at the Sundance Canyon trailhead.

RATING
Tender
DISTANCE
3.7 km to Sundance Canyon trailhead
TIME
1 hour return
ELEVATION GAIN
30 m (100 ft)
MAP
82 O/4 Banff

ACCESS
Cave and Basin, Banff.
From the bridge over the Bow River on Banff Avenue, follow the signs to the Cave and Basin at the west end of Cave Avenue.

29 MAP 21
HEALY CREEK ROAD

The Healy Creek road, which is the original access road to Sunshine Village from Banff, is a smooth gravel road covered with pine needles. Healy Creek is bridged. There is little view from the pine forest but it is still pleasant cycling and the trail is useful as a shortcut to Sunshine Village. There is a beaver pond at the east end of the trail. The Brewster Creek Fire Road forks to the south 1.9 km from the west access.

RATING
Tender
DISTANCE
4.8 km
TIME
1 - 2 hours round trip
ELEVATION GAIN
30 m (100 ft)
MAP
82 O/4 Banff

EAST ACCESS
Cave and Basin, Banff. Cycle the Sundance trail (#28) to a gated road at the 2.9 km point.

WEST ACCESS
From Banff's west interchange, drive 9 km west on the Trans-Canada Highway and turn south on the Sunshine Village Road. Park at the trailhead 0.8 km south of the Trans-Canada Highway.

30 MAP 21
BREWSTER CREEK FIRE ROAD & ALLENBY PASS

The entire Brewster Creek trail from the Healy Creek Road to Bryant Creek via Allenby Pass (32.3 km) has been designated as a bicycle route. The initial 8.8 km-long Brewster Creek Fire Road is a smooth gravel road that provides easy cycling. Frequently driven by outfitters, it rises steadily through pine forest that allows for little in the way of a view - a hoodoo at 6.9 km is one of the few points of interest. A private outfitter's cabin marks the end of the road.

Past the cabin, the trail is rough and muddy and deteriorates as it approaches Allenby Pass. The trail receives a great deal of horse traffic which constantly churns up the clay soils creating pits which fill up with water with every passing shower. When I tried to cycle to Allenby Pass my back tire collected so much mud that it stopped turning as I pushed the bike. The entire Spray - Brewster loop (about 95 km) has been ridden in one day in drier weather, but it is a rough and very difficult trip.

RATING
Tender to end of road
Tough to Bryant Creek
DISTANCE
8.8 km to end of road
32.3 km to Bryant Creek
TIME
2 - 3 hours return to cabin
ELEVATION GAIN
185 m (600 ft)
MAP
82 O/4 Banff

EAST ACCESS
Park at Cave and Basin in Banff. Cycle 2.9 km on the paved Sundance trail (#28) to Healy Creek Road (#29). Cycle 2.9 km to the junction with Brewster Creek Fire Road that is signed "Allenby Pass".

WEST ACCESS
From Banff's west interchange, drive 9 km west along the Trans-Canada Highway and turn south on the Sunshine Village Road. Park at the trailhead 0.8 km south of the Trans-Canada Highway. Cycle 1.9 km east on the Healy Creek road to the junction with Brewster Creek Fire Road that is signed "Allenby Pass".

75

31 MAP 21
BRYANT CREEK TO
ASSINIBOINE MEADOWS

This cycling trip starts at Canyon Dam at Spray Lakes Reservoir, goes up Bryant Creek, and crosses over Assiniboine Pass to Lake Magog in Assiniboine Provincial Park, British Columbia. It is one of the most popular backcountry bicycle trips in the Canadian Rockies and you can expect to meet numerous hikers, bicycles and horses, especially on long weekends. Normally it takes 2 or 3 days to cover this route by backpacking. Cycling into this area allows you to spend more time hiking the many trails and attractions including Wonder Pass, Owl Lake, Allenby Pass and Assiniboine Park. All trails in this area are well marked and signed and easy to follow.

CANYON DAM TO BRYANT CREEK - The first 14.6 km are easy cycling on road. 1.8 km of rough, rutted four-wheel drive road is followed by 5.3 km of smooth gravel road along the lakeshore. The Trail Centre at the boundary of Banff National Park is a simple kiosk with trail maps. It lies at the junction of the Bryant Creek and Watridge Lake trails.

BRYANT CREEK - The 7.5 km of narrow dirt road along Bryant Creek can be a joy to cycle when it is dry. If it is wet, you can expect it to be muddy and rough due to heavy horse travel. The Bryant Creek Warden Cabin, Public Shelter and campground are clustered in the meadows near the junction with the Marvel Lake trail. The shelter is quite busy throughout the summer.

The next 7.2 km of trail leading to Assiniboine Pass is the difficult part of the trip. The road narrows to a rutted single track which splits into a horse trail and a hiking trail 3 km past the Bryant Creek Warden Cabin. Take the horse trail which crosses Bryant Creek - it is shorter, wider and easier to travel. Knee-deep ruts and a rock slide from Cascade Rock will force you to walk the bike. Push or carry the bike for the last kilometre to the convoluted confines of Assiniboine Pass.

RATING
Terrific - dry weather only
DISTANCE
24.3 km to Magog Lake
TIME
6 - 8 hours round trip
ELEVATION GAIN
490 m (1600 ft)
MAPS
82 J/14 Spray Lakes Reservoir
82 J/13 Mount Assiniboine

ACCESS
From Canmore, drive 17.6 km south on Smith-Dorrien–Spray Trail (S.R. 742) through Whiteman Gap to the dam on Spray Lakes Reservoir. Drive across the dam and continue 16 km south along the Spray Lakes West Road and park at Canyon Dam. The last 10 km of the Spray Lakes West Road are not well maintained and the road is rough and rocky. The trail is a dirt road west of Canyon Dam and the spillway.

ASSINIBOINE - Just when you are ready to give up mountain biking forever, you will be rewarded by the smooth, level, surfaced trails through the meadows of Assiniboine Provincial Park. Severe problems with braided, muddy, eroding trails led the B.C. Parks Service to surface these trails with shale. It is an easy 2.5 km cycle through alpine meadows and clumps of fir to the campground on Lake Magog. The lake is overshadowed by Mount Assiniboine and its ring of glaciers. Inquire about afternoon tea at the rustic Assiniboine Lodge. The Naiset Cabins are four small log cabins operated as alpine huts by B.C. Provincial Parks which are run on a first come, first served basis in summer. There is a small fee for their use.

With a little pushing, the trail past Naiset Cabins can be cycled to Wonder Pass, a wild, barren, windswept pass with a panoramic view of Assiniboine meadows.

On the return trip, you must walk your bike down Assiniboine Pass but after that it is an easy and pleasant ride out Bryant Creek. We received looks of disbelief when we talked to backpackers at Lake Magog at 5 pm. They were amazed that we had left Canyon Dam at 1 pm and that we would be back in Calgary by 10 pm.

CYCLING OPTION
MARVEL LAKE

The 2 km of trail from Bryant Creek Warden Cabin to Marvel Lake has been designated as a bicycle trail. The trail is a single track through mature spruce forest with some roots and is popular with people who want to fish these beautiful green waters. This large backcountry lake is surrounded by steep slopes and avalanche tracks.

Jo-Ann Draper in Assiniboine meadows.

32 MAP 21
SPRAY RIVER FIRE ROAD

The Spray Lakes Fire Road is a high-grade, gravel road for its entire length from the Banff Springs Hotel to Canyon Dam on Spray Lakes Reservoir. The gentle grade provides easy cycling in either direction. Several large washouts which formed in the spring of 1986 may not be repaired.

A youth hostel, four campsites on the Spray River Fire Road and campsites along the Spray Lakes West Road provide many options for an overnight trip.

The north end of the road follows the Spray River through mature spruce forest and provides access to the Spray River Hostel, so expect to meet hikers along the way. The junction with Goat Creek trail, a dirt road, is well marked. Shortly after, the Spray River Fire Road bends to the west to follow the river through a gap between Sulphur Mountain and the Goat Range.

Near Rink's Camp there is a dramatic view of the Goat Range to the east. The north end of the range is composed of reddish shale which has formed good meadows. The south end is limestone which does not form good meadows partly because of the high concentration of calcium which is toxic to most plants. North of the Mount Fortune campsite there may be several washouts depending on the spring meltwaters and the park's activity in maintaining the road.

South of Mount Fortune camp, wide gravel flats along the river provide a view south to Mount Shark and Tent Ridge. Several avalanche tracks cross the road before it joins the road from Canyon Dam to Bryant Creek. This unmarked junction in the middle of a hill is easy to miss if you are travelling from the Canyon Dam end. To the left, 1.8 km of rough, rutted, dirt road leads to the trailhead at Canyon Dam and a clear view of Spray Lakes Reservoir.

RATING
Tender
DISTANCE
40.6 km
TIME
3 - 6 hours one way
ELEVATION GAIN
335 m (1100 ft)
MAPS
82 O/4 Banff
82 O/3 Canmore
82 J/14 Spray Lakes
Reservoir

NORTH ACCESS
The trailhead lies south of the Banff Springs Hotel on the south side of the Bow River in Banff. A gated gravel road leaves the south side of the upper parking lot.

SOUTH ACCESS
From Canmore, drive 17.6 km south on Smith-Dorrien-Spray Trail through Whiteman Gap to the dam on Spray Lakes Reservoir. Cross the dam and continue 16 km south along the Spray Lakes West Road and park at Canyon Dam. The last 10 km of the Spray Lakes West Road are not well maintained and the road is rough and rocky. The trail is a dirt road west of Canyon Dam.

CYCLING OPTIONS
An 84.4 km loop trip with easy cycling can be made in conjunction with the Spray Lakes West Road and Goat Creek (#33). The loop can be shortened to 64.8 km by starting from Goat Creek or Canyon Dam in the Spray Valley.

78

33 MAP 21
GOAT CREEK

The Goat Creek trail connects the Smith-Dorrien—Spray Trail (S.R. 742) and the Spray River Fire Road (#32).

The trail is a smooth, slightly vegetated, dirt and gravel road travelling through pine and spruce forest. It follows Goat Creek between Mount Rundle and the Goat Range to a bridged crossing of the Spray River near the junction with Spray River Fire Road. The east end of the trail is poorly maintained and there may be some awkward creek crossings where culverts have been washed out.

RATING
Tender
DISTANCE
9.4 km one way
TIME
1 hour one way
ELEVATION GAIN
150 m (495 ft)
MAPS
82 O/3 Canmore
82 O/4 Banff

EAST ACCESS
The Goat Creek trailhead is on the west side of the Smith-Dorrien—Spray Trail (S.R. 742), 9.0 km south of Canmore past Whiteman Gap.

WEST ACCESS
Spray River Fire Road (#32), 6.1 km south of Banff. The junction is well marked.

CYCLING OPTIONS
Loop trips can be made with the Spray River Fire Road (#32) and Spray Lakes West Road (64.8 km), with the Trans-Canada Highway via Banff and Canmore (54.2 km), or with the Rundle Riverside trail (#34) and the Smith-Dorrien—Spray Trail (S.R. 742).

Spray River Fire Road with Goat Range in the background.

79

34 MAP 21
RUNDLE RIVERSIDE TRAIL

The Rundle Riverside trail follows the south bank of the Bow River to the park boundary and there joins the Banff trail, a wide gravelled trail which leads to the Canmore Nordic Centre (#35). The Rundle Riverside trail is a difficult, technical single track that is a challenge for the more dedicated and determined cyclist. The trail is being upgraded and may be more rideable when it is completed.

The gates at the entrance of the golf course may be locked at night. It may be a good idea to park at the Bow Falls lookout and cycle along the golf course road to the trailhead.

RATING
Very Tough
DISTANCE
8.3 km to park boundary
TIME
4 - 6 hours return trip
ELEVATION GAIN
nil
MAP
82 O/3 Canmore

ACCESS
In Banff, follow the golf course road to the bridge over the Spray River below the Banff Springs Hotel. Drive past the bridge for 2.5 km and take the fork to the right. Park at a gravel pulloff 1.2 km from the fork.

Odlum Creek logging road. Highwood Range in the background. ⇨
Claudia Ederle, Jo-Ann Draper, Nancy Gas

Mountain Biking can be very hard on the thumbs.

KANANASKIS
COUNTRY

35 MAP 21
CANMORE NORDIC CENTRE

In the summer of 1987 the Canmore Nordic Centre will be open for the first time for mountain biking and hiking. The management expects that the majority of the 56 km of ski trails will be available for cycling. The two-lane gravelled Banff trail runs from the Nordic Centre 6 km to the boundary of Banff National Park and connects with the Rundle Riverside trail (#34). Other trails do not have as firm a surface but they will offer more interesting riding terrain.

The lodge is open in the summer and provides lockers, showers and a cafeteria. Trail maps are available at the lodge. The Canmore Nordic Centre will be of special interest to groups holding races and individuals who want convenient trails for training.

For more information phone the Nordic Centre at 403-678-2400.

RATING
Tender-tough
DISTANCE
56 km of trails
MAP
820/3 Canmore

ACCESS
From Canmore follow the Smith-Dorrien–Spray Lakes Trail (S.R. 742) for 4.1 km to the Nordic Centre.

Jo-Ann Draper demonstrating good downhill riding technique.

WATRIDGE LAKE

Watridge Lake trail is a level dirt and gravel logging road connecting Mount Shark trailhead to a point close to Watridge Lake. All creeks are bridged and the trail is well marked.

The logging road provides easy cycling. It starts as a gravel road and gradually mellows to a dirt logging road as it passes through cutblocks at the foot of Tent Ridge. The area still looks quite rough since this was one of the last areas to be logged in the Spray Valley. Tent Ridge came close to becoming a large ski resort and a venue for some of the alpine events at the '88 Winter Olympics. It is an excellent area for telemark skiing because of high snowfall and open slopes on the upper part of Tent Ridge. Many of the logging roads have been cleared and marked as part of a cross country ski trail system. Mount Fortune is the most prominent peak on the north shore of Spray Lakes Reservoir, while Mount Turner and Mount Morrison stand to the west in Banff National Park.

The logging road ends 0.6 km from Watridge Lake, and a rough, single track crossed by tree roots carries on. You may prefer to leave your bike at the end of the road and walk to the lake. Surrounded by mature spruce and fir forest, Watridge Lake is renowned for its cutthroat trout.

NOTE: The hiking trail from Watridge Lake to the Trail Centre on Bryant Creek has become a popular access route for hikers travelling up Bryant Creek to Mount Assiniboine. This option is 1 km shorter than the Canyon Dam access and saves bouncing your car over the rough Spray Lakes West Road. However, the 2 km of trail from Watridge Lake to Trail Centre is unrideable on a mountain bike because of rough, wet, muddy and thoroughly unpleasant trail conditions. Parks are considering building a connecting trail suitable for horse and bicycle travel. There are tentative plans to eventually close the southern part of the Spray Lakes West Road after the Spray Lakes campground is expanded and improved. While the Spray Lakes West road is still open, the Canyon Dam access is the preferred route for backcountry cyclists headed up Bryant Creek.

RATING
Tender
DISTANCE
4.0 km
TIME
1 hour round trip
ELEVATION GAIN
nil
MAP
82 J/14 Spray Lakes
Reservoir

ACCESS
Drive to the Mount Shark Recreation Area access road which joins the Smith-Dorrien–Spray Trail (S.R. 742) 38.8 km south of Canmore and 28.6 km north of the junction with Kananaskis Trail (Hwy. 40). Drive 5.4 km west to the Mount Shark trailhead.

HIKING OPTION
KARST SPRING
From Watridge Lake, a hiking trail crosses the outlet and leads 0.8 km south to a huge spring which is the source of Watridge Creek. Karst Spring, which is one of the largest of its kind in North America, bubbles from a dark, mossy nook on the north slope of Mount Shark. The source of the spring remains a mystery. Karst springs can develop into large caves, but the process has been delayed by the long periods of glaciation in the Canadian Rockies.
For more information on these trails consult the Kananaskis Country Trail Guide

MAP 22

37 MAP 22
CHESTER LAKE

The Chester Lake trail is a logging road and hiking trail that rises steadily to a beautiful mountain lake. It was a difficult route to follow until it was marked and signed by Alberta Parks.

This short 2.3 km cycle up a logging road gives you access to the signed hiking trail that branches off the road. Rocky washouts and the steeper hills make it a challenging ride.

Parks management have restricted cycling on the rest of the route to avoid conflicts with hikers. Starting in mature forest, the hiking trail is rough and crossed by roots. It later improves as it passes through meadows with clumps of larch, fir and willow.

Chester Lake is an impressive mountain lake surrounded by high peaks. It is rumoured to have some large arctic char that are almost impossible to catch.

RATING
Tough
DISTANCE
2.3 km biking; 2.2 km hiking
TIME
2 hours round trip
ELEVATION GAIN
305 m (1000 ft)
MAP
82 J/14 Spray Lakes Reservoir

ACCESS
Chester Lake trailhead is located on the east side of Smith-Dorrien–Spray Trail (S.R. 742), 45.0 km south of Canmore and 22.4 north of the junction with Kananaskis Lakes Trail (Hwy. 40).

HIKING OPTIONS
UPPER CHESTER CREEK
The trail continues past Chester Lake to a high alpine valley where a rough trail leads to the summit of The Fortress.

THREE LAKES VALLEY
The trail leading north from Chester Lakes leads to the next drainage which flows from Mount Galatea. It is an alpine cirque with three paternoster lakes.

RUMMEL LAKE
An alpine traverse with no trail will get you to another impressive alpine lake two valleys north of Chester Lake.
For more information on these trails consult the Kananaskis Country Trail Guide.

Chester Lake at the outlet
photo Gillean Daffern

85

38 MAP 22
BURSTALL LAKES

The Burstall Pass trail is an old logging road and hiking trail leading to a pass between Kananaskis Country and the upper Spray Valley in Banff National Park. Cycling is permitted only as far as the gravel flats west of Burstall Lakes. Bikes are sometimes used by telemark skiers to speed up access to Robertson Glacier in the fall. Skis can be strapped to the head tube and seat tube. Make sure the bindings are far enough back to clear your thighs when peddling.

The trail starts by crossing the dam on the south end of Mud Lake. The dam forces Mud Lake to flow both north to Spray Lakes and south to Lower Kananaskis Lake. Either way, the water flows through several power generating stations on its way to Calgary. Follow the signs for Burstall Pass past several forks along 3.0 km of good dirt road winding through spruce and fir forest. There are several other logging roads near the lakes to explore. From the end of the road there is 400 m of rough trail crossed with tree roots to endure before the trail emerges out of the forest onto the glacial outwash from the Robertson Glacier.

RATING
Tender
DISTANCE
3.0 km to end of road
TIME
1 hour round trip
ELEVATION GAIN
60 m (200 ft)
MAP
82 J/14 Spray Lakes
Reservoir

ACCESS
The trail starts at Burstall Pass trailhead on the west side of Smith-Dorrien–Spray Trail (S.R. 742) at Mud Lake, 45 km south of Canmore and 22.4 km north of the junction with Kananaskis Lakes Trail (Hwy. 40).

HIKING OPTION
BURSTALL PASS
A hiking trail crosses the gravel flats and climbs up the valley through subalpine forest and meadows to spectacular rambling expanses of meadow at the pass. There is a deep sinkhole on the west side of the pass and a view of colourful Leman Lake and Spray Pass.
For more information on these trails consult the Kananaskis Country Trail Guide

SMITH-DORRIEN MOUNTAIN BIKE TRAIL SYSTEM

Also referred to as the Sawmill Trails, these trails are a mixed bag of old logging roads that traverse the lower slopes of the Kananaskis Range through open spruce forest and cutblocks. Alberta Parks and members of the Foothills Nordic Ski Club cleared logs off the roads to provide rustic ski touring routes which are marked with colour-coded circles nailed to trees. There are striking views to the rugged Spray Mountains on the west side of the Smith-Dorrien Valley.

I have only cycled a few of these trails so I cannot give you a thorough description. The folks at Alberta Parks assure me that they are all passable by bicycle. You can expect the entire range of trail quality from smooth and easy to loose and rough with many short steep sections. The longest rideable loop around the outside of the trail system measures 18.5 km. There are more logging roads here than the ones marked on the map. Some of the trails are more suitable for cross country skiing than mountain biking but it is an interesting place to explore.

RATING
Tender - tough
DISTANCE
32 km of trails
MAP
82 J/14 Spray Lakes
Reservoir

ACCESS
The trail system is accessed from the Sawmill trailhead on the east side of Smith-Dorrien–Spray Trail (S.R. 742) 51.4 km south of Canmore and 16 km north of the junction with Kananaskis Lakes Trail. It can also be reached from the Chester Lake trailhead (#37).

HIKING OPTION
HEADWALL LAKES
Cycling the yellow trail provides access to the Headwall Lakes hiking trail. It travels through a rugged and beautiful valley with waterfalls and meadows. For more information on these trails consult the Kananaskis Country Trail Guide

40 MAP 23
SKOGAN PASS

The road over Skogan Pass was built to access the powerline, but fortunately only 5 km of the road shares the powerline right-of-way. Skogan Pass was named by Don Gardner while designing the Ribbon Creek cross country ski trails. It is a Norwegian word meaning a magic forest with elves and trolls.

The lower part of the trail is a gravel road which crosses the Nakiska Ski Area. Stay right at Marmot Creek.

Where the road reaches the powerline, a detour can be made to the Lookout on Hummingbird Plume Hill. After this junction the road degenerates to a dirt surface and continues to climb through pine forest and cutblocks. The location of the pass is deceptive because the trail reaches a high point 100 m above the actual pass. The open pine forest carpeted with grouseberries makes this one of the more appealing parts of the ride. From the pass there is a good view of the Three Sisters and the Canmore corridor .

The north side of the pass provides a good downhill ride under the powerline - a fitting reward for the pushing and hard riding. The road is rocky in places but is mostly smooth and gravelled. Watch for a trail sign indicating the connecting road to Pigeon Mountain ski area.

RATING
Tough
TIME
4 hours one way
DISTANCE
19 km
ELEVATION GAIN
665 m (2170 ft)
ELEVATION LOSS
760 m (2500 ft)
MAPS
82 J/14 Spray Lakes Reservoir
82 O/3 Canmore

SOUTH ACCESS
From the Trans-Canada Highway drive south on Kananaskis Trail (Hwy. 40) for 23.3 km to the Ribbon Creek Recreation Area access road. Park at the Nakiska Ski Area parking lot.

NORTH ACCESS
From Pigeon Mountain, the truck stop at Deadman Flat on the Trans-Canada Highway, drive south from the interchange for about 1.5 km to a parking lot near the abandoned Pigeon Mountain Ski Area. The trail follows a dirt road south to the powerline.

CYCLING OPTIONS
You can either arrange a car shuttle or cycle back to your starting point via the Trans-Canada Highway and Kananaskis Trail (Hwy. 40) for a round trip distance of approximately 63 km. Loop trips can also be made with Jewel Pass (#41) and/or the Stoney trail (#42).

MAP 23

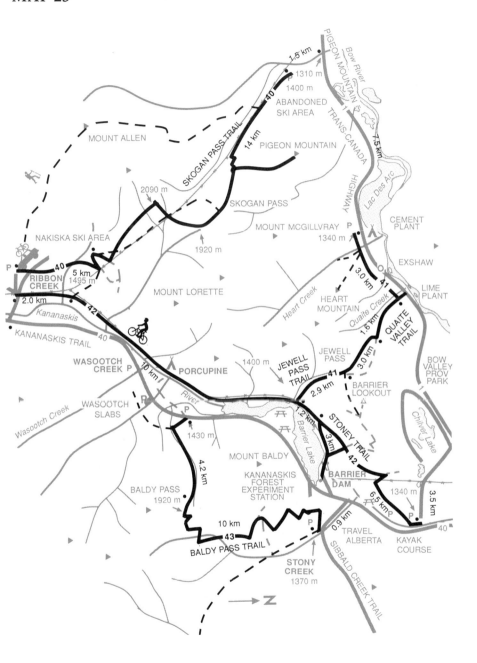

89

41 MAP 23
JEWELL PASS

This route connects the Bow Valley with the Kananaskis Valley at Barrier Lake via the Quaite Valley and the Jewell Pass trails. The gentler slopes of the Quaite Valley trail make it more enjoyable to ride this route from north to south. Both trails are popular with hikers so please be considerate.

QUAITE VALLEY - From Heart Creek trailhead a wide, smooth, rolling, single track parallels the Trans-Canada Highway for 3 km. At Quaite Creek it joins the the Quaite Valley trail, a good gravel road which passes a large backcountry group campsite at a meadow. Don't miss the right turn immediately past the group camp. The aspens, dogwoods and willows put on a good show of colours here in the fall. Push and peddle up to Jewell Pass.

JEWELL PASS - Pines block the view from this low pass and the junction of five trails causes confusion despite the trail sign. The Jewell Pass trail is the smooth, single track leading south-east. The lower parts of the trail present some tricky technical riding past boulders. Walk or carry the bike down a short steep stretch. Jewell Falls, on the west side of the deep narrow valley, can be seen from the trail. Further down, a bench above the creek provides a good view of Barrier Lake and Mount Baldy. The Jewell Pass trail joins the Stoney trail at the powerline near a small secluded bay on Barrier Lake.

RATING
Tough
DISTANCE
10.5 km one way
TIME
1 - 2 hours one way
ELEVATION GAIN
280 m (920 ft)
ELEVATION LOSS
220 m (720 ft)
MAP
82 O/3 Canmore

HEART CREEK ACCESS
From the Lac Des Arc interchange on the Trans-Canada Highway, follow the signs to Heart Creek trailhead parking lot on the south side of the highway.

CYCLING OPTIONS
Loop trips can be made with the Stoney trail (#42) and the Trans-Canada Highway (30.4 km) or the Stoney trail (#42) and Skogan Pass (#40) (50.5 km).

STONEY TRAIL (BOW VALLEY PARK TO RIBBON CREEK)

Stoney trail follows the route of a major powerline on the west side of the Kananaskis River from Bow Valley Provincial Park to the Ribbon Creek trailhead. It is smooth gravel and dirt road most of the way. Chinook winds tend to keep this route dry - we have ridden this trail in dry conditions as early as April and as late as November. Loop trips can be make in conjunction with Skogan Pass (#40), Jewell Pass (#41) or Kananaskis Trail (Hwy. 40). It also connects with the Evan-Thomas paved bike path (#45) from Ribbon Creek to Wedge Pond.

From the north access, cycle a dirt road frequented by horses to a old log bridge crossing the Kananaskis River. This is part of the first road into the Kananaskis Valley. Built in 1934 during the Depression, it ran from Seebe to a camp for the unemployed. The camp later became a prisoner of war camp for German prisoners during World War II and is now the Kananaskis Forest Experiment Station. Backtrack for about 200 m to an unmarked, vegetated gravel road leading to the south. This road soon crosses the powerline, veers to the north and makes you feel like you must be going the wrong way. West of the powerline, a fork to the south continues on smooth dirt and gravel road through mixed forest and meadows past the access road to Barrier Lake Lookout and joins the powerline on the north shore of Barrier Lake.

From Barrier Lake the Stoney trail follows the powerline for over 12 km to Ribbon Creek. It is a rolling dirt and gravel road that passes a series of beaver ponds along the river. The grey slabs of Mount Lorette, a popular rock climbing area, rise to the north. The Ribbon Creek Recreation Area provides access to Kananaskis Trail (Hwy. 40), Skogan Pass (#40) and Evan-Thomas bike path (#45).

RATING
Tender
DISTANCE
19.7 km
TIME
2 - 4 hours one way
ELEVATION GAIN
245 m (800 ft)
MAPS
82 O/3 Canmore
82 J/14 Spray Lakes Reservoir

NORTH ACCESS
From the Seebe interchange on the Trans-Canada Highway drive south for 3.5 km on a gravel road into the southern part of Bow Valley Provincial Park. The road passes under a major powerline and continues through a meadow to a water treatment reservoir near the Kananaskis River.

SOUTH ACCESS
From the Trans-Canada Highway, drive 23.3 km south to the access road to Ribbon Creek Recreation Area. Follow the signs for 1.4 km to the Ribbon Creek trailhead parking lot.

43 MAP 23
BALDY PASS LOOP

The Baldy Pass loop involves a push up to Baldy Pass, a downhill ride to Stony Creek trailhead and a return on Kananaskis Trail (Hwy. 40). Crossing the pass from west to east takes advantage of a good downhill ride on the east side. Horses are not allowed on this trail.

The Baldy Pass trail starts on the east side of Kananaskis Trail (Hwy. 40) in a cutblock grown over with willows which demonstrates some of the difficulties of regenerating commercially valuable species in the eastern slopes. After 1 km the smooth, single track joins a good logging road which soon fades out in the dry, rocky creek bed. There is a clear view to Nakiska Ski Area on Mount Allan. The rest of the trip to the pass is a steep push up a single track through a narrow valley. The trail passes scree slopes and a large avalanche track just below the pass. The transition of trees across the rocky pass shows their reaction to microclimates. Pine and spruce form a typical subalpine forest on the west side, whitebark pine occupies the rocky windswept ridge and subalpine fir grows on the cooler east side of the pass.

Push up the east side of the ridge for 250 m following the cairns. A 1 km single track on the east side of the pass joins a logging road and the good downhill riding begins - a 10 km-long gravel road ending at Stony Creek trailhead. The road passes through several cutblocks and gives a clear view of Baldy Mountain to the west.

From Stony Creek it is an 8 km ride along the wide paved shoulders of Kananaskis Trail past Barrier Lake to the Baldy Pass trailhead.

RATING
Terrific
DISTANCE
22.2 km round trip
TIME
3 - 5 hours round trip
ELEVATION GAIN
550 m (1800 ft)
MAPS
82 J/14 Spray Lakes Reservoir
82 O/3 Canmore

ACCESS
Park at the access road for the Porcupine group camp on the west side of Kananaskis Trail (Hwy. 40), 15.1 km south of the Trans-Canada Highway. The signed trail starts on the east side of the highway.

Jo-Ann Draper at Evan-Thomas Pass.
Mount Evan-Thomas in background.
"Gathering strength to complete a ⇨
long tiring ride."

EVAN-THOMAS CREEK

The exploration road provides access to Evan-Thomas Pass for climbs and exploration in the Fisher or Opal Ranges. The first 9 km offers good cycling on a gravel road. The next 5 km deteriorates and the road becomes narrow, rough and wet in places. Willow thickets, washed out road and boggy ground alternate with sections of good road. There is a good place to camp north of the pass.

The grey limestone wall of Mount Evan-Thomas towers above the pass to the west. The highest peak in the Opal Range, it is named after Rear Admiral Evan-Thomas who fought at Jutland in 1916. The sharp, jagged outline of this peak is caused by erosion of nearly vertical slabs of limestone. The mountain which dominates the view to the east is Fisher Peak.

RATING
Tough
DISTANCE
14 km to Evans Thomas Pass
TIME
6 - 8 hours return
ELEVATION GAIN
610 m (2000 ft)
MAP
82 J/14 Spray Lakes Reservoir

ACCESS
From the Trans-Canada Highway drive south on Kananaskis Trail (Hwy. 40) for 27.7 km to the Evan-Thomas Creek trailhead. The trailhead parking area is 300 m north of the creek.

HIKING OPTION
From Evan-Thomas Pass, a hike through the willows and meadows can be made to a small lake below Mount Evan-Thomas. The road on the north side of Evan-Thomas Pass fades out and a steep narrow trail continues to the Little Elbow River. I discovered the hard way that it is totally unsuitable for a bicycle.
For more information on these trails consult the Kananaskis Country Trail Guide

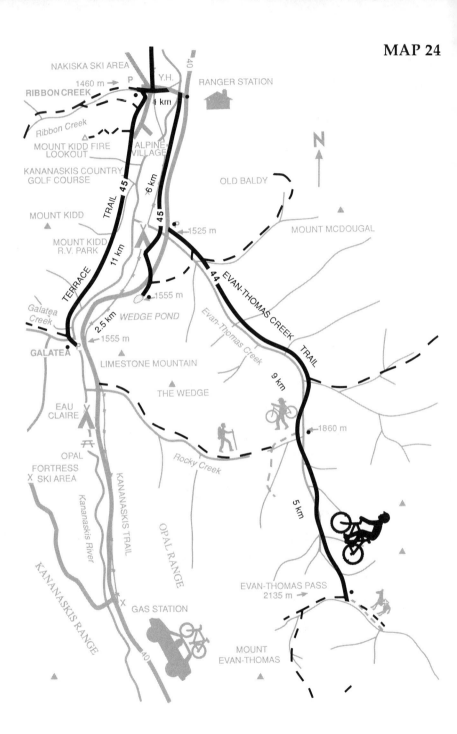

MAP 24

NAKISKA SKI AREA

1460 m →

RIBBON CREEK

P   Y.H.

RANGER STATION

1 km

Ribbon Creek

MOUNT KIDD FIRE
LOOKOUT

ALPINE
VILLAGE

KANANASKIS COUNTRY
GOLF COURSE

OLD BALDY

6 km

TRAIL 45

45

1525 m

MOUNT MCDOUGAL

MOUNT KIDD

MOUNT KIDD
R.V. PARK

11 km

44

EVAN-THOMAS CREEK

TERRACE

1555 m

Galatea
Creek

2.5 km   *WEDGE POND*

Evan-Thomas Creek

TRAIL

GALATEA

1555 m

9 km

LIMESTONE MOUNTAIN

THE WEDGE

EAU
CLAIRE

1860 m

OPAL
FORTRESS
X SKI AREA

Rocky Creek

KANANASKIS TRAIL

Kananaskis River

OPAL RANGE

5 km

KANANASKIS RANGE

GAS STATION

EVAN-THOMAS PASS
2135 m →

40

MOUNT
EVAN-THOMAS

45 MAP 24
TERRACE TRAIL & EVAN - THOMAS BIKE PATH LOOP

Terrace hiking trail and the Evan-Thomas paved bicycle path make an interesting loop trip when combined with a section of Highway 40. Hikers frequent Terrace trail and may be difficult to spot because of tight blind corners. If you don't have the courtesy to watch out for hikers, then do the rest of us a favour and don't ride this trail.

TERRACE TRAIL is a smooth, single track of dirt and gravel covered in pine needles. It is graded "tough" because of the tight winding corners that present fun technical riding. Two creeks from Mount Kidd have created wide boulder creek beds you will want to walk the bike across. The creeks are almost always very small. From the Galatea trailhead, cross the suspension bridge across the Kananaskis River. The trail follows the edge of a terrace on the west side of the river offering a good view of the Kananaskis Valley. You can hear people smacking balls on the golf course. The white sand traps, green grass and manicured water traps make an interesting contrast with the wild tangle of the beaver ponds. The Wedge, Limestone Mountain, Fisher Peak and Mount McDougall can be seen on the east side of the valley while the grey wall and gigantic folds of Mount Kidd rise immediately to the west. Ribbon Creek Alpine Village provides a refreshment stop 1 km south of the Ribbon Creek trailhead.

The EVAN-THOMAS bike path leads 7 km from the Ribbon Creek trailhead to Wedge Pond. A wide paved path winding through pine forest, it passes the Kananaskis Golf Course and the Mount Kidd Recreational Vehicle Park where you can stop for refreshments and a soak in a hot tub. The pavement ends at Wedge Pond, a small lake that was dredged to provide soil for the golf course. Like many man-made lakes at other recreational areas in Kananaskis, it went through a stage as an unattractive pit caused by natural resource extraction. It has since been lined with a water resistant bottom, stocked with fish and landscaped to create a recreational resource.

RATING
Tough
DISTANCE
20.5 km round trip
TIME
2 - 3 hours round trip
ELEVATION GAIN
95 m (310 ft)
MAP
82 J/14 Spray Lakes Reservoir

SOUTH ACCESS
Start at the Galatea trailhead on the west side of Kananaskis Trail (Hwy. 40), 33 km south of the Trans-Canada Highway.

NORTH ACCESS
The Ribbon Creek Recreation Area is on the west side of Kananaskis Trail (Hwy. 40), 23.3 km south of the Trans-Canada Highway. Drive 1 km west to the Ribbon Creek trailhead.

46 MAP 25
POCATERRA -
WHISKEY JACK LOOP

This loop trip follows Pocaterra and Whiskey Jack trails, former fire lookout access roads, then returns via Wheeler and Lodgepole bicycle paths. It is a pleasant trip accessible from the various campgrounds along the Kananaskis Lakes Trail. All junctions are well signed and all creek crossings are bridged. This route is marked on a detailed backcountry map available at the Visitor Centre.

POCATERRA trail starts at a large marsh, a relatively uncommon feature in the Rockies. There is an active beaver lodge and great blue herons feed among the sedges.

Most of Pocaterra trail is a smooth, vegetated road offering dramatic views of Mount Wintour and the Opal Range to the east. The first 1.2 km wanders along Pocaterra Creek to the Pocaterra Group camp. Cross the confusion of the group camp and pick up the road in the south-east corner. The road continues through willows and meadows and crosses numerous wide bridges built to accommodate a double tracked ski trail. The road rises above the creek at the edge of a canyon and climbs steadily through pine forest, but you can still peddle up it in low gear. The trail is covered in pine needles and the forest floor with grouseberries.

At 8.3 km Pocaterra trail joins the Kananaskis Fire Lookout access road, a well-travelled gravel road which branches from Kananaskis Trail (Hwy. 40).

WHISKEY JACK - At 9.8 km, Whiskey Jack trail branches to the west. This old road was recently bulldozed and graded to smooth out deep erosion gullies. It is a steep and sometimes rough descent. Watch out for hikers. Whiskey Jack descends to Boulton Campground, crosses the baseball diamond meadow and emerges at the parking lot by the Trading Post.

RATING
Tough
DISTANCE
25.0 km round trip
TIME
3 - 5 hours round trip
ELEVATION GAIN
320 m (1040 ft)
MAP
82 J/14 Kananaskis Lakes

ACCESS
The trailhead is located at Pocaterra Hut near the intersection of Smith-Dorrien–Spray Trail (S.R. 742) and Kananaskis Lakes Trail. Pocaterra trail is an old road hidden in the trees a few metres south-east of the Hut.

BIKE PATHS - The return trip is on Wheeler and Lodgepole trails which are wide, paved bicycle paths providing easy enjoyable cycling through pine forest along the valley floor. They are all signed, but can be confusing where they wander through Boulton and Elkwood campgrounds. En route, pass a restaurant, showers, outdoor theatre and Visitor Centre.

MAP 25

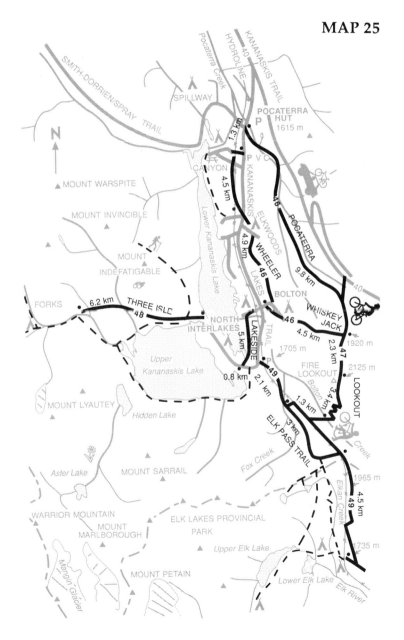

97

47 MAP 25
POCATERRA – LOOKOUT LOOP

Pocaterra trail can be combined with a traverse of the Kananaskis Fire Lookout hill on the Lookout trail. Elk Pass, Lakeside, Wheeler and Lodgepole trails return you to Pocaterra Hut. The north end of this loop is described in the Pocaterra -Whiskeyjack Loop (#46).

LOOKOUT - Cycle Pocaterra trail to the Kananaskis Fire Lookout access road, also known as Lookout trail, which rises 205 m in 2.3 km. It is a smooth gravel road that you can grind up in low gear to Kananaskis Fire Lookout which provides a panoramic view. You have the option of either coasting back down the smooth Lookout road or tackling the rough road that continues south to the Hydroline road. This 3.4 km stretch of rough, dirt bulldozer track can scarcely be called a road. It is horrible when wet and some people would find it an unpleasant flirt with the dirt at the best of times. The one saving grace is that it is a steep downhill most of the way to the Hydroline.

The HYDROLINE is a smooth dirt road in the wide clearing under the powerline that crosses Elk Pass. It drops into the steep Fox Creek Valley and joins the ELK PASS trail (#49). This smooth dirt road climbs out of the other side of the valley and then provides a smooth descent to the Elk Pass trailhead.

BIKE PATHS - From the Elk Pass trailhead cycle west (left) on the pavement of the Kananaskis Lakes Trail (road) to Lakeside trail at the Mount Sarrail trailhead. Lakeside trail, a wide paved bike path, meanders through solid pine forest along the Lower Kananaskis Lake. The west end of the bike path crosses the trickle of water that used to be the upper Kananaskis River. It flowed from the Upper Lake to the Lower Lake over a spectacular waterfall that was sacrificed for the hydroelectric development. Farther on, the path wanders through Lower Lake campground and climbs up to Boulton campground where you can pick up the Wheeler bike path. Follow Wheeler and Lodgepole bike paths back to Pocaterra Hut.

RATING
Terrific - dry weather only
DISTANCE
35.4 km round trip
TIME
4 - 6 hours round trip
ELEVATION GAIN
600 m (1970 ft)
MAP
82 J/14 Kananaskis Lakes

ACCESS
The trailhead is located at Pocaterra Hut near the intersection of Smith - Dorrien—Spray Trail (S.R. #742) and Kananaskis Lakes Trail. Pocaterra trail is an old road hidden in the trees a few metres south-east of the Hut.

48 MAP 25
THREE ISLE FIRE ROAD

The Three Isle Fire Road along the north shore of Upper Kananaskis Lake is a short but interesting road that ends at the Kananaskis River. Parks may be installing bicycle racks at the end of the road. Cycling the road can give you a head start if you are hiking onward to the forks, or the North or South Kananaskis passes. Both these hiking trails are off limits for cycling.

The road was built in 1967 to help fight a forest fire that swept across the south slopes of Mount Indefatigable (also known as Mount Unpronounceable). The grey trunks of the fire killed trees are still standing.

Although it is mostly a dirt road, it becomes rocky where it crosses a huge rock slide which fell from Mount Indefatigable. The bedding plane where the rock fractured is clearly visible. The glaciation of this valley created a steep face on the mountain. It is possible that the pressure of the ice weakened the underlying layers of rock and when the glacier receded, the face was no longer supported by the ice. Water seeping along the bedding plane probably weakened the rock further until a series of massive rock slides fell down the slope and into what is now the Upper Kananaskis Lake. Research on the site indicates that six major slide events have occurred, the last one occurring about 200 years ago. The volume of the slide debris is several times larger than that of the Frank Slide. The slope is expected to slide again within the next few centuries.

RATING
Tender
DISTANCE
6.2 km one way to Kananaskis River
TIME
1 - 2 hours return
ELEVATION GAIN
nil
MAP
82 J/14 Kananaskis Lakes

ACCESS
From the Trans-Canada Highway, drive 50.4 km south on Kananaskis Trail (Hwy. 40) and turn west onto Kananaskis Lakes Trail (paved road). Drive 14 km to North Interlakes trailhead at the end of the Kananaskis Lakes Trail.

HIKING OPTIONS
For more information on these trails consult the Kananaskis Country Trail Guide

49 MAP 25
ELK PASS & ELK LAKES PROVINCIAL PARK

The Elk Pass trail provides a route from the Kananaskis Lakes area over Elk Pass to Elk Lakes Provincial Park in British Columbia.

ELK PASS TRAIL - From Elk Pass trailhead push and peddle up the smooth dirt road through spruce and pine forest. The road passes under the powerline and descends into the steep Fox Creek Valley.

After crossing the bridge over Fox Creek you are presented with a choice. The left fork of the road is the Hydroline trail. The Elk Pass trail, the vegetated dirt road to the right, offers a more interesting route along Fox Creek but the upper part of it has a loose dirt surface that is harder to peddle along. The two routes join at the summit of Elk Pass. Avoid the boggy hiking trail that branches off Elk Pass trail and follows Elkan Creek down the south side of Elk Pass.

HYDROLINE TRAIL- From the bridge over Fox Creek, the left fork which is a steep road climbs out of the creek valley and joins the powerline that crosses Elk Pass. The Hydroline is a smooth dirt road that offers easier cycling than the Elk Pass trail. A good option is to cycle up the smoother Hydroline and return on the more interesting Elk Pass trail.

Elk Pass is a low, wide rolling break in the Divide that was considered along with Kicking Horse Pass as a route for the Trans-Canada CPR railway. Moose and elk are common even though they are seldom seen. There are areas on the pass that look like barnyards because of the trampling of elk hooves.

ELK PASS TO ELK LAKES PROVINCIAL PARK - The road under the powerline offers a fast, smooth descent to the large meadow at the boundary of Elk Lakes Provincial Park. Two rough cabins stand at the edge of the meadow.

RATING
Tough - dry weather only
DISTANCE
9.6 km to Elk Lakes Park entrance
TIME
4 - 6 hours return
ELEVATION GAIN
275 m (900 ft)
MAP
82 J/11

ACCESS
From the Trans-Canada Highway, drive 50.4 km south on Kananaskis Trail (Hwy. 40) and turn west onto Kananaskis Lakes Trail (paved road). Drive 11.5 km to Elk Lakes trailhead parking.

HIKING OPTION
ELK LAKES
Cycling over Elk Pass allows you to take a day trip into the beautiful and relatively wild Elk Lakes Provincial Park. An 8.4 km hiking trail, too narrow and rough for cycling, leads past both Lower and Upper Elk Lakes, along gravel flats to spectacular Petain Falls and up the steep headwall to the cirque at the foot of the Petain Glacier. Elk Lakes provide good fishing but a British Columbia fishing permit is required. For more information on these trails consult the Kananaskis Country Trail Guide

50 MAP 26
EAGLE HILL TRAIL

This rough trail ends at a lookout north-west of Sibbald Flats. It is a combination of road and rough trail through valley bottom pine and poplar forest and is fairly well marked with red diamonds. You'll find it a bit like riding through a barnyard because of the numerous cattle ranging through the wide clearings which were made to improve grazing. It is best to walk the last kilometre up the lookout hill which overlooks the Stony Indian reservation in the Bow Valley.

The best part of the trail is the sweat lodge and Sun Dance lodge in the meadow near the start. Multi-coloured cloths hanging from poplar trees mark the site of the Sun Dances. The sweat lodge, a small dome of willows, stands behind it. To have a sweat bath, a frame of willows is covered with hides or a tarp. Stones are heated in an outside fire until red hot, then dumped into a pit in the centre of the lodge. Pouring water over the rocks controls the temperature in the lodge. I have used a sweat lodge on many occasions by using a tent fly for the cover. Nothing feels better after a hard day on the trail. The interpretive brochure reads: "Please respect the Indian's religious symbol, leave the site undisturbed, and allow the changing seasons to do their work."

RATING
Tough - dry weather only
DISTANCE
7.5 km one way
TIME
3 - 4 hours round trip
ELEVATION GAIN
180 m (600 ft)
MAP
82 O/2 Jumpingpound

ACCESS
Sibbald Lake Recreation Area day use parking lot on Sibbald Creek Trail (Hwy. 68).

MAP 26

51 MAP 27
JUMPINGPOUND RIDGE LOOP

The Jumpingpound Ridge trail is a spectacular traverse of a high sandstone ridge. The trail is good to ride in either direction, but riding south to north provides excellent downhill riding through meadows on the north slope of the ridge.

Cycle the good dirt road along Canyon Creek for 0.7 km to the Jumpingpound Ridge trail which is marked with red diamonds. Push the bike for 2 km up switchbacks through pine forest and small meadows brimming with wildflowers. There are some springs here where you can fill up your water bottles for the dry trip over the ridge.

RATING
Terrific - dry weather only
DISTANCE
21.8 km loop
TIME
4 - 6 hours round trip
ELEVATION GAIN
630 m (2060 ft)
MAP
82 J/15 Bragg Creek

SOUTH ACCESS
The trail starts on the east side of Powderface Trail (gravel road), 100 m north of Canyon Creek, 15 km north of Elbow Falls Trail (Hwy. 66), and 20 km south of Sibbald Creek Trail (Hwy. 68).

NORTH ACCESS
The north end of the Jumpingpound Ridge trail is located on the east side of Powderface Trail (gravel road), 24.3 km north of Elbow Falls Trail (Hwy. 66) and 10.7 km south of Sibbald Creek Trail (Hwy. 68).

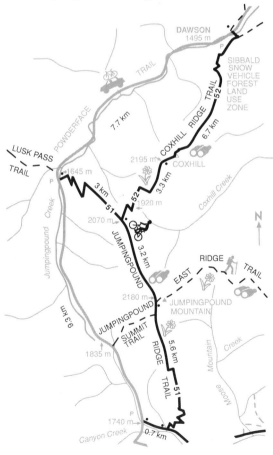

MAP 27

The trail levels out in pine forest carpeted with grouseberries. This high pine forest around 2000 m always reminds me of the Wind River Range in Wyoming and the Sierras in California - "Sierra North" I call it. The summit meadows provide a view of the rocky desert of the Fisher Range and Compression Ridge to the west.

The north slope of the ridge provides some of the most spectacular ridge riding in the Rockies. Stone cairns mark the smooth trail through meadows. Massive Moose Mountain stands to the east beyond the sinuous east ridge of Jumpingpound Mountain, while to the west lies a sweeping panorama of the Front Ranges of the Rockies. A smooth switchbacking trail descends the north end of the ridge back to the road. Please ride as if there was a horse around every corner.

It is a 9.3 km ride on the gravel of Powderface Trail back to Canyon Creek.

Classic ridge ride on Jumpingpound Ridge.

52 MAP 27
COX HILL RIDGE LOOP

The work is hard on this trail but the rewards are plenty. The summit is spectacular and the ride down the north side guaranteed to shorten the life of your brake pads.

Push up the switchbacks at the north end of the Jumpingpound Ridge trail on sidecut single track through solid pine forest. The trail meets Cox Hill Ridge trail to left before climbing out of the trees. Cox Hill Ridge trail immediately drops 150 m in 1 km on steep smooth trail to a col between Jumpingpound Mountain and Cox Hill. All this elevation must be regained by pushing up the steep south side of Cox Hill. In the summer of '86, the trail had been cut and brushed but no tread had been cut. One kilometre from the col the trail emerges out of the trees onto steep summit meadows. Continue pushing up the rocky meadows along the ridge for 1.5 km to the summit. There is a dazzling view of Jumpingpound Mountain's east ridge and Moose Mountain to the south and range after range of the Rockies to the north-west.

After a short walk along the summit ridge find the smooth sidecut track leading down the north-east ridge. In 6.7 km the trail drops 700 m (2300 ft), the longest continuous rideable drop I have found yet. You never go very fast on this winding technical trail, but please watch for horseback riders anyway.

From Dawson day-use area it is a 7.7 km ride on the gravel of Powderface Trail back to the trailhead.

RATING
Terrific - dry weather only
DISTANCE
20.7 km loop
TIME
4 - 7 hours round trip
ELEVATION GAIN
850 m (3000 ft)
MAPS
82 J/15 Bragg Creek
82 O/2 Jumpingpound

ACCESS
The trail starts on the east side of Powderface Trail (gravel road), 24.3 km north of Elbow Falls Trail (Hwy. 66) and 10.7 km south of Sibbald Creek Trail (Hwy. 68). Cox Hill Ridge trail branches off the north end of Jumpingpound Ridge trail (#51).

CYCLING OPTION
For strong and energetic riders there is the option of starting at Canyon Creek and riding Jumpingpound Ridge and Cox Hill in one loop trip of 36.5 km with 1055 m (3460 ft) of elevation gain.

Gerhardt Lepp in a mudhole churned up by cattle on the Telephone Trail ⇨

104

53 MAP 28
TELEPHONE LOOP

Telephone trail, the longest of the West Bragg ski trails, follows old exploration roads covered with pine needles that provide easy cycling.

The terrain consists of low rolling foothills with no major peaks or landmarks. Although the trail is marked with ski trail signs, there are several junctions with seismic roads where it is easy to get lost. The "S bend" is one place in particular where many people lose track of the route and cycle down the wrong seismic line. The trail makes a loop to the north around a low hill. On the north slope of the hill, be prepared for a wet, boggy area where cattle have ploughed up a mud hole. The trail crosses a low pass and returns south to the meadows along the Bragg Creek road. Part of the road has been "put to bed" but is still rideable. The trail follows part of a telephone line that once connected the Elbow and Jumpingpound Ranger stations. Insulators that supported the line can still be seen hanging from trees.

There are many seismic lines and exploration roads in this area that provide interesting riding but little scenic interest. Navigation is tricky; don't forget the compass.

RATING
Tough - dry weather only
DISTANCE
16 km round trip
TIME
4 - 5 hours return
ELEVATION GAIN
215 m (700 ft)
MAPS
82 J/15 Bragg Creek
82 O/2 Jumpingpound Creek

ACCESS
In Bragg Creek, cross the bridge over the Elbow River and drive 10 km west to the West Bragg picnic area. There is a large parking lot on the north side of the road for cross country ski parking. A map and sign marks the trailhead.

MAP 28

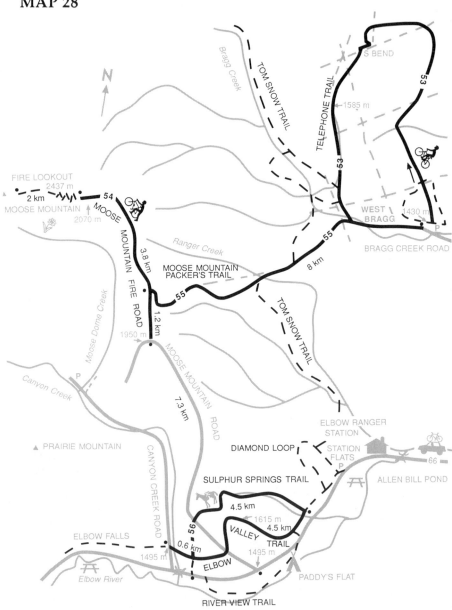

54 MAP 28
MOOSE MOUNTAIN FIRE LOOKOUT ROAD

The Moose Mountain Road is usually open to vehicles during the summer but has been closed periodically to prevent the public from interfering with gas drilling operations on the mountain. It allows you to drive 455 m above the valley floor and gain access to the fire road which continues to climb up the south-east ridge of Moose Mountain.

The fire road offers easy cycling along a spectacular mountain ridge without the effort of pushing up a long hill - it's a good family trip. Brilliant green meadows fill the openings in the fir and pine forest. The deep canyon of Moose Dome Creek drops away to the west. Ahead of you, Moose Mountain is part of a huge domed structure of limestone and one of the most prominent peaks visible from Calgary. The shape makes it a natural reservoir for gas, hence the many wells on the mountain.

The road's smooth shale surface and gentle rise enable strong cyclists to peddle most of the way to the meadow below the switchbacks. From here it is a further 2 km hike with 367 m of elevation gain to the fire lookout. The road switchbacks up a bare rocky slope and eventually fades into an exposed pack trail that makes the final approach to the windswept summit. Water is available early in the season from a spring a short walk down the north slope of the summit.

On the return ride watch out for hikers since this is such a popular trail. Square blocks of shale on the road may attack your front wheel. These vicious creatures are in the same family as the snow snake.

RATING
Tender
DISTANCE
5 km to switchbacks
TIME
2 - 3 hours return
ELEVATION GAIN
120 m (400 ft) to meadow below switchbacks
MAP
82 J/15 Bragg Creek

ACCESS
From Bragg Creek, drive 17.6 km west on Elbow Falls Trail (Hwy. 66) and turn north onto Moose Mountain Road (0.7 km west of Paddy's Flat campground). Drive north for 7.3 km and park at a gated fire road leading to the north.

55 MAP 28
MOOSE MOUNTAIN PACKER'S TRAIL

This steep, unmarked route is only for experienced gonzo riders. It drops 520 m from the Moose Mountain Fire Lookout Road to the West Bragg ski trail parking lot. There is no point in doing the trail in the opposite direction. You can either arrange a car shuttle by leaving a vehicle at West Bragg ski parking or cycle the 35.4 km back to Moose Mountain Fire Road via Bragg Creek. If you cycle the round trip, do not forget the 455 m of elevation gain going up the Moose Mountain Road.

Look for an unmarked trail to the east, 1.2 km from the gate at the start of the Moose Mountain Fire Road. It starts as a smooth and pleasant single track - part of the original horse packer's trail that provided access to the Moose Mountain Fire Lookout. The easy riding ends as the trail drops down a steep and rough seismic line. Where the seismic line continues straight over a desperately steep, dome shaped hill, a road to the south provides a more agreeable fat-tire route. This overgrown, rutted, seldom used road wanders east through cut blocks to a gravelled, gas well access road. Follow the access road to the left, back to West Bragg ski parking.

Beware of dastardly diagonal ditches; erosion gullies waiting to trap the front tire of the unsuspecting.

RATING
Terrific - dry weather only
DISTANCE
8.0 km
TIME
2 - 3 hours
ELEVATION LOSS
520 m (1700 ft)
MAP
82 J/15 Bragg Creek

ACCESS
From Bragg Creek, drive 17.6 km west on Elbow Falls Trail (Hwy. 66) and turn north onto Moose Mountain Road (0.7 km west of Paddy's Flat campground). Drive north for 7.3 km and park at a gated fire road leading to the north. Cycle the Moose Mountain Fire Lookout trail (#54) to the 1.2 km point.

108

SULPHUR SPRINGS LOOP

The Sulphur Springs trail in combination with the Elbow Valley trail makes an interesting short loop. The trail was named for sulphurous waters that seep out of natural springs along the trail. Much of the trail is a smooth, rolling, single track through open pine forest. It receives very little horse traffic but be careful to watch for them anyway. Both the Sulphur Springs loop and the Diamond T loop were the site of the 1986 Ridley's Summer Solstice Mountain Bike Race.

Start the trip by crossing shallow, rocky Canyon Creek. Push and peddle up the steep sidecut trail to a large meadow where the Elbow Valley trail meets the Sulphur Springs trail - this junction is easy to miss despite the sign. The meadow at the junction offers a view of Prairie, Powderface, Forgetmenot and Nihahi ridges rolling off to the west. After a hill the trail drops to a well site on the Moose Mountain Road. It's all downhill from here along Sulphur Springs Creek back to the Elbow Valley trail.

The Elbow Valley trail has similar hilly terrain requiring some pushing. If you are feeling lazy you can miss out this section and cycle back on the pavement of Elbow Falls Trail (Hwy. 66).

RATING
Tough
DISTANCE
10.2 km round trip
TIME
2 - 4 hours round trip
ELEVATION GAIN
305 m (1000 ft)
MAP
82 J/15 Bragg Creek

ACCESS
From Bragg Creek, drive 19.6 km west on Elbow Falls Trail (Hwy. 66) to the Canyon Creek Road. The Elbow Valley trail crosses the Canyon Creek Road about 500 m north of the junction. Look for the red squares marking the trail.

MAP 29

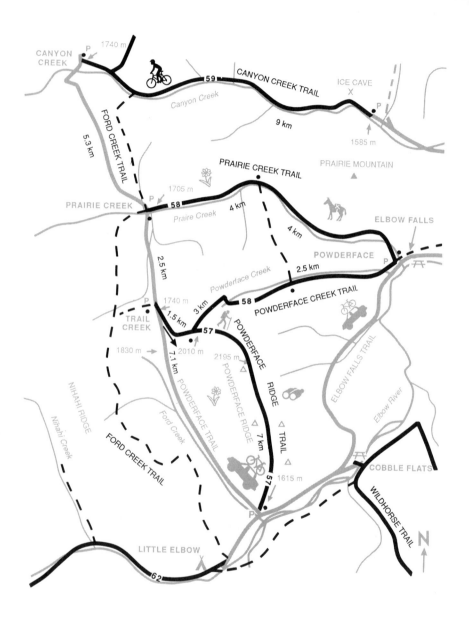

57 MAP 29
POWDERFACE RIDGE LOOP

This trip involves a two hour push to the open meadows on Powderface Ridge and a long, steep descent back to Powderface Trail (road). It's hard work but the more intrepid rider will find it great fun. The ridge provides an excellent view of Calgary and the foothills, as well as Nihahi ridge to the west.

Push up the switchbacks of Powderface Creek trail for 1.5 hours to Powderface Pass and the start of the Powderface Ridge trail. Another 0.5 hours of pushing your fat tires through meadows gets you to the top of the ridge. Unfortunately, most of the ridge is too rocky for cycling and it is often too windy. A new trail, built to avoid the worst of the rocks along the summit ridge, descends the east side of the ridge to a grassy spur.

The steep downhill ride starts in the meadows on the east side of the ridge and winds through the pine forest for a total drop of 500 m in 3 km. If you enjoy skiing through the trees, you'll enjoy this downhill ride on a soft carpet of pine needles. Wearing a helmet is strongly recommended. Watch for horses.

You may want to use a power assisted mountain bike brake. If your hands get sore from squeezing the brakes, wrap an elastic band around the handlebar and the front brake lever. By changing the number of wraps, you can adjust the brake to the proper drag to control your descent.

Return to the trailhead by cycling 7.1 km north on the gravel surface of Powderface Trail (road).

RATING
Terrific - dry weather only
DISTANCE
15.6 km round trip
TIME
6 hours round trip
ELEVATION GAIN
670 m (2200 ft)
MAP
82 J/15 Bragg Creek

ACCESS
From Bragg Creek, drive west on the Elbow Falls Trail (Hwy. 66) for 31 km to the junction with Powderface Trail (gravel road). Drive north on Powderface Trail for 7.1 km to the start of the Powderface Creek trail.

Gerhardt Lepp grinding the gears up Powderface Ridge. Nihahi Ridge on the left.

58 MAP 29
PRAIRIE CREEK –
POWDERFACE CREEK LOOP

This loop trip includes Prairie Creek trail, Powderface Trail (road) and Powderface Creek trail. Most of the trail has a one metre- wide tread with a smooth dirt surface. The cycling is of intermediate difficulty except for the western part of Powderface Creek trail which is a steep push. All of the trails are signed and marked with red diamonds.

PRAIRIE CREEK trail is anything but prairie-like. Much of it is cut into the sides of this steep, pine forested valley. Some pushing is required as the trail alternately climbs the valley side and drops back down to the creek. The trail receives little use despite the fact that it is a rather interesting valley. There is a rocky canyon at the 2.5 km point and a striking view of Compression Ridge in the Fisher Range to the west.

POWDERFACE TRAIL, a narrow, winding, gravel road serves as a north-south link between Prairie Creek and Powderface Creek trails.

The POWDERFACE CREEK trail starts by climbing 270 vertical m in 1.5 km from the Powderface Trail (road) to Powderface Pass on the north end of Powderface Ridge. It takes at least 1.5 hours to push a bike up the switchbacks to the top of the col. You are rewarded by an excellent view of Nihahi Ridge to the west.

The Powderface Creek trail now descends into dark spruce forest and joins an exploration road about 1 km east of the pass. The east side of the pass is a steep descent that requires good braking power. Lower down, the dirt road is less steep as it descends through valley meadows and pine forest back to Powderface trailhead on Highway 66.

RATING
Terrific
DISTANCE
17.5 km loop
TIME
4 -6 hours round trip
ELEVATION GAIN
490 m (1600 ft)
MAP
2 J/15 Bragg Creek

ACCESS
From Bragg Creek, drive 22.6 km west on Elbow Falls Trail (Hwy. 66). Park at the Powderface trailhead west of Elbow Falls.
This loop trip could also be accessed by driving north on Powderface Trail (gravel road) to where Prairie Creek or Powderface Creek trails meet the road.

The parking lot is also the trailhead for the Moose Mountain ice cave, reached by following a trail which angles up the scree slope to a large vertical slot in the mountain side. The cave has an ice floor year round. Unfortunately, it has been subject to vandalism and litter from thoughtless people.

Note that the road up Moose Dome Creek has been closed due to the hazards of hydrogen sulphide gas. In the winter of 85 - 86 a sour gas pipeline and compressor station was built along Lower Canyon Creek.

The Canyon Creek trail starts as a rocky four-wheel drive road which disappears in the creek bed. The first 3 km of the trail crosses and recrosses the creek bed in a dramatic, steep-walled limestone canyon. It's not an early season trip. The water fades to a trickle in the heat of summer but can be a torrent in the spring. Eventually, the trail emerges from the canyon and the cobbles give way to a good trail and later on a dirt road which winds through meadows, willows and pines.

RATING
Tough - dry weather only
DISTANCE
9 km one way
TIME
2 - 3 hours one way
ELEVATION GAIN
155 m (500 ft)
MAP
82 J/15 Bragg Creek

ACCESS
From Bragg Creek, drive 19.6 km west on the Elbow Falls Trail (Hwy. 66) to Canyon Creek. Follow the road up Canyon Creek for 6 km to a parking lot at the end of the driveable road.

CYCLING OPTION
A loop trip can be made with either the Prairie Creek trail (31.3 km) or Powderface Creek trail (32.8 km). See trail # 58. Use Powderface Trail (road) as the connecting link since Ford Creek trail has been badly eroded by cattle.

A typical view of Canyon Creek - photo Gillean Daffern

60 MAP 30
QUIRK CREEK - WILDHORSE LOOP

This is a trail you'll want to ride again for its gradual uphill climb and enjoyable downhill ride.

QUIRK CREEK ROAD - Ford the Elbow River and cycle the road that goes down the Elbow River and turns up Quirk Creek. This is a high-grade gravel road which provides pleasant cycling all the way up the valley through meadows along the creek. Motor bikes may be encountered since this is part of the McLean Creek Off-Highway Vehicle Zone. More vehicles use the road in the fall when the gate at Cobble Flats is left open.

At 8 km there is a bridge over Quirk Creek. An interesting side trip can be made to the canyon on Threepoint Creek by crossing the bridge and cycling south for 3 km on a good dirt road to the canyon. This black shale canyon reaches a depth of 140 m and the walls are etched with the trails of bighorn sheep.

WILDHORSE - Return on the Wildhorse trail which crosses Howard Creek and Mac Creek. It provides good trail cycling on wide, smooth trail. At Mac Creek you can see the signs of a rock slide which fell from Forgetmenot Ridge. Most of the debris is buried under the meadow. The last 5 km is a winding drop of 150 m through pine forest and meadow back to the Elbow River. Watch for horses.

RATING
Tough
DISTANCE
20 km loop
TIME
3 - 4 hours round trip
ELEVATION GAIN
250 m (820 ft)
MAPS
82 J/15 Mount Rae

ACCESS
From Bragg Creek drive west on Elbow Falls Trail (Hwy. 66) for 29 km to Cobble Flats picnic area, 2 km east of Powderface Trail (road). From the picnic area you will see an obvious road which crosses the Elbow River which is a wide, shallow braided stream at this point.

MAP 30

114

ELBOW LAKE &
TOMBSTONE LAKES

The headwaters of the Elbow River contains six subalpine lakes - Elbow Lake, Tombstone Lakes, Rae Lake and Sheep Lakes - each of which can be reached on a biking and hiking day trip. Tombstone backcountry campground is an excellent base camp for exploratory rides.

From the trailhead, an old dirt and gravel road rises steeply and some pushing is required to reach Elbow Lake, one of the most popular day hikes in the area. A backcountry campground is hidden in the spruce forest on the south side of the lake. The road crosses the scree slopes along the north shore to the meadows east of Elbow Lake which are alive with wildflowers in June and July. A fire which swept through the valley many years ago has left the area unusually open.

The sometimes rocky road descends the upper Elbow Valley to the forks, the junction of Big Elbow, Little Elbow and Sheep trails. Little Elbow trail, the smooth gravel road that climbs toward Little Elbow Pass, leads to the signed junction with Tombstone Lakes trail. Alberta Parks has prohibited cycling on the Tombstone Lakes trail so leave your bike and walk a rough and rutted hiking trail to the two lakes nestled into a cirque on Mount Tombstone. En route, the trail passes through one of the most magnificent stands of larch in Kananaskis Country. The dark green waters of the lower lake attract many trout fishermen but the upper lake is proof of the porosity of the limestone rock. During late summer it often drains and becomes a mud flat.

RATING
Tough
DISTANCE
 9.0 km to Tombstone Lakes
TIME
3 - 4 hours one way
ELEVATION GAIN
305 m (1000 ft)
ELEVATION LOSS
120 M (400 ft)
MAPS
82 J/11 Kananaskis Lakes
82 J/10 Mount Rae

ACCESS
The trail starts at the Elbow Pass trailhead on the east side of Kananaskis Trail (Hwy. 40), 62.7 km south of the Trans-Canada Highway and 5 km north of Highwood Pass.

HIKING / CYCLING OPTION
SHEEP TRAIL (#70)
A smooth gravel road leads south to the pass at the head of the Sheep River. Sheep Lakes can be reached from the pass by hiking north through wide, rolling meadows and clumps of larch. Rae Lake to the south-west is best reached from a point 1 km north of the pass.

62 MAP 31
ELBOW LOOP

The Elbow Loop is a classic mountain bike route along former four-wheel drive roads. The route follows Little Elbow trail over Little Elbow Pass to the forks and returns via Big Elbow trail.

LITTLE ELBOW - The first 12.5 km of dirt and gravel road along the Little Elbow River is easy undulating cycling. From Mount Romulus backcountry campsite, the next 8 km of road climbs 425 m to Little Elbow Pass. Rocky washouts force you to walk your bike through the boulders. There is a striking view of Mount Romulus to the north. From the larches and meadows at the summit of the pass, the Misty Range comes into view. En route, a rough hiking trail 1 km north of the pass provides a side trip to the Tombstone Lakes. The road on the south side of the pass is an excellent downhill run on smooth gravel road. Watch for Big Elbow trail, a road to the left before the bottom of the hill.

RATING
Tough
DISTANCE
41.5 km round trip
TIME
6 - 8 hours round trip
ELEVATION GAIN
670 m (2200 ft)
MAPS
82 J/10 Mount Rae
82 J/15 Bragg Creek

ACCESS
From Bragg Creek, drive west on Elbow Falls Trail (Hwy. 66) for 32 km to Little Elbow Recreation Area. Trailhead parking is provided near the campground entrance. Cycle along the campground road to the trailhead which is a gated dirt road at the west end of the campground.

Colynn Kerr crossing the west fork of the Little Elbow. Mount Romulus in background.

116

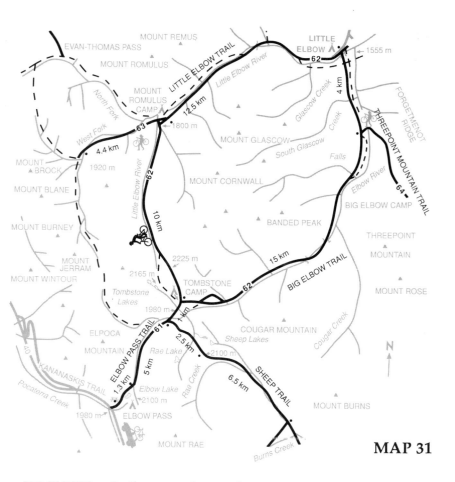

MAP 31

BIG ELBOW trail offers somewhat rougher cycling. A steep hill 1 km from the junction can be avoided by following the less rigorous sidecut trail around the hill. The next obstacle occurs where the old road and the river become one and the same. You can either wade down the river or walk the narrow trail that bypasses it. Two deep river crossings farther on are both bridged. The lower 11.5 km of the Big Elbow trail is easy cycling on gravel road with occasional washed out sections where spring runoff crosses the road. Pine, poplar and meadows have make slow progress in colonizing the gravel flats along the Elbow River. A suspension bridge crosses the Little Elbow River and returns you to the trailhead.

117

63 MAP 31
WEST FORK
OF LITTLE ELBOW

Although the rough seismic road up the West Fork of the Little Elbow River is not a great cycle trip by itself, it provides access to the Opal Range for hiking and climbing.

This side trip starts as an obvious rocky, dirt road leading to Mount Romulus backcountry campground. After a shallow ford of the south fork of Little Elbow River, the road climbs a short steep hill. Further on, a bend in the river forces you to ford the West Fork twice more. The last ford adds adversity to the trip with a high gravel bank that makes the crossing difficult. The road plunges into the river again at the 4.4 km point and the road bed and creek bed become one.

Mount Blane is the dramatic dogtooth peak to the west. This peak fascinated me until I climbed it in 1980 while working as a park ranger. The guidebook described it as having "good" rock. All that Dave Zevick and I found were removable hand holds and a helicopter pad where a climber with a broken leg had been evacuated several years earlier. We didn't know we had reached the top until we started going down the other side - I could barely see my partner on the other end of the rope because of a heavy fog.

RATING
Tough - dry weather only
DISTANCE
4.4 km one way
TIME
2 hours return
ELEVATION GAIN
120 m (395 ft)
MAPS
82 J/15 Bragg Creek
82 J/14 Spray Lakes
Reservoir
82 J/11 Kananaskis Lakes

ACCESS
From Mount Romulus backcountry campground at the 12.5 km point on Little Elbow trail (#62).

HIKING OPTION
Seldom travelled trails in this beautiful valley lead north to a pass by Mount Evan-Thomas and south to a pass between Mount Jerram and Mount Tombstone. If you plan to hike to the Opal Range, remember that grizzlies often graze in the meadows below these peaks.
For more information on these trails consult the Kananaskis Country Trail Guide

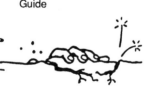

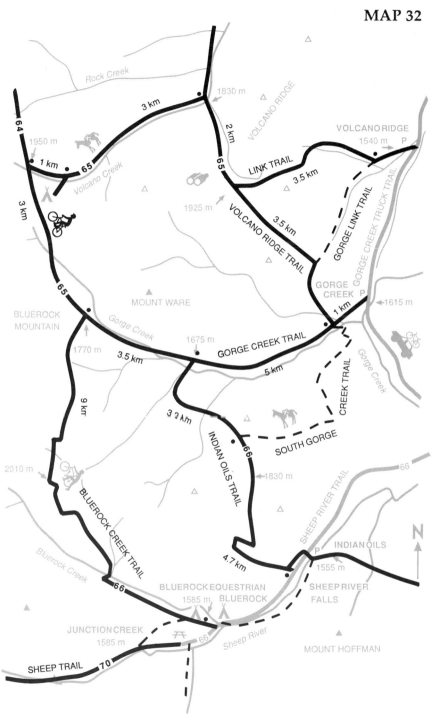

MAP 32

Rock Creek

3 km

1830 m

VOLCANO RIDGE

2 km

VOLCANO RIDGE

1540 m P

64

1950 m

1 km

65

65

LINK TRAIL

3.5 km

Volcano Creek

1925 m

VOLCANO RIDGE TRAIL

3.5 km

GORGE LINK TRAIL

GORGE CREEK TRUCK TRAIL

3 km

GORGE CREEK P

65

1 km

1615 m

BLUEROCK
MOUNTAIN

MOUNT WARE

Gorge Creek

1675 m

GORGE CREEK TRAIL

Gorge Creek

1770 m

3.5 km

5 km

CREEK TRAIL

9 km

3.2 km

SOUTH GORGE

2010 m

INDIAN OILS TRAIL

66

1830 m

SHEEP RIVER TRAIL

66

BLUEROCK CREEK TRAIL

Bluerock Creek

INDIAN OILS

N

66

4.7 km

1555 m

BLUEROCK EQUESTRIAN

SHEEP RIVER
FALLS

1585 m   BLUEROCK

JUNCTION CREEK

1585 m

66

Sheep River

MOUNT HOFFMAN

SHEEP TRAIL   70

64 MAP 31, 32
THREEPOINT MOUNTAIN TRAIL

The Threepoint Mountain trail is a single track connecting Big Elbow trail (#62) and Volcano Creek trail (#65) across the drainage divide between the Elbow and Sheep valleys. The trail varies from rough to smooth.

From Big Elbow trail, ford the wide, shallow braided channels of the Elbow River. Push up a pine-covered ridge at the base of Forgetmenot Mountain. Mount Cornwall can be seen to the west at the head of a deeply glaciated valley with a waterfall. After crossing the divide, the single track joins an exploration road along Threepoint Creek but soon leaves the road, crosses the creek and continues south. Below Threepoint Mountain and Mount Rose the trail passes through meadows and patches of subalpine forest before joining Volcano Creek and Gorge Creek trails.

RATING
Tough
DISTANCE
9.2 km from Big Elbow trail to Volcano Creek trail
TIME
2 - 3 hours one way
ELEVATION GAIN
335 m (1000 ft)
MAPS
82 J/15 Bragg Creek 82 J/10 Mount Rae

ACCESS
Big Elbow Trail (#62), 4.5 km south of Little Elbow Recreation Area. At the junction of the road and horse trail, cycle north on the horse trail, a rough, single track, for 0.8 km to the signed junction with the Threepoint Mountain trail.

CYCLING OPTION
A long loop trip of 44 km could be ridden in combination with Volcano Creek, Volcano Ridge and Wildhorse trails.

"You don't really ride down such steep slopes do you?" Kathy Staniland on the Gorge Creek trail near Bluerock Mountain

65 MAP 32
VOLCANO RIDGE
GORGE CREEK LOOP

This is one of the most enjoyable loops in the Sheep River Valley. It is well marked with trail signs and is mostly on exploration roads although a bit of everything will be encountered.

VOLCANO RIDGE - Cycle 1 km west on Gorge Creek trail to a stream crossing in a meadow where the trail forks on the west side of the creek. The Volcano Ridge trail is the obvious trail up the creek through the meadow. Follow this wide trail up a ridge through open lodgepole pine. From the top of the ridge there is a spectacular view of Bluerock Mountain to the west. A good downhill ride on a seismic line leads in 2 km to the junction with the Volcano Creek trail. This hill has numerous ditches known as tank traps built to control erosion. Several years of weathering have rounded them off and they make interesting jumps.

VOLCANO CREEK - Cycle the narrow trail through the willows and meadows of Volcano Creek. The trail is little more than an improved cow path but offers smooth cycling. Bluerock Mountain looms above the west end of the valley.

GORGE CREEK From the Gorge Creek trail you get a good view of the deep canyon on Gorge Creek between Mount Rose and Bluerock Mountain. The toughest part of the trail is the steep shale path cut into the hillside along the canyon. It requires some fancy footwork - you may even wish you had wings! The next obstacle is the steep uphill section on the other side of the valley. The tree roots and ruts in this mature spruce forest make for difficult travel.

Don't be discouraged because after the Bluerock trail junction there is some excellent downhill riding for 8.5 km through meadows, side cut trails and smooth road at the edge of Gorge Creek. Problems have occurred on the Gorge Creek trail with bicycles meeting horses where the trail traverses a ledge on the side of a little gorge. Dismount when meeting horses and if necessary get off of the trail to let them pass.

RATING
Tough
DISTANCE
23 km
TIME
5 - 6 hours round trip
ELEVATION GAIN
430 m (1400 ft)
MAP
82 J/10 Mt. Rae

ACCESS
Drive west from Turner Valley on Sheep River Trail (S.R. 546) for 30.5 km to the Gorge Creek Truck Trail (gravel road) located between the Sheep Ranger Station and Gorge Creek. Drive north on this narrow gravel road for 4 km to the Gorge Creek trailhead.

BLUEROCK – INDIAN OILS LOOP

This is a trail for tough riders with strong minds and good techniques on switchbacks. The beautiful foothill country makes tackling this rugged trip worthwhile.

BLUEROCK trail begins as a good logging road but deteriorates quickly in the first kilometre. A narrow trail with steep switchbacks winds down to the foot bridge crossing Bluerock Creek. After the bridge, the trail begins gaining elevation immediately. Push up the shoulder of Bluerock Mountain. Enjoy the view and the steep downhill ride to the meadow along Gorge Creek. Gorge Creek trail offers pleasant, flat cycling with numerous creek crossings. Watch for cattle and horseback riders.

Although INDIAN OILS trail is marked by a sign, it is easy to miss. Indian Oils is a more moderate trail which climbs over a ridge with some steep sections. The trail switchbacks down from the ridge through open, dry hillside to a short rolling section of trail leading back to the Sheep River road.

RATING
Terrific - dry weather only
DISTANCE
23.4 km round trip
TIME
7 - 8 hours round trip
ELEVATION GAIN
750 m (2450 ft)
MAP
82 J/10 Mount Rae

ACCESS
From Turner Valley drive 37 km west up the Sheep River Trail (S.R. 546) to the Bluerock equestrian staging area on the north side of the road.

Lunch break on Volcano Ridge with Bluerock Mountain in the background.   Jeff Gruttz

67 MAP 33
VOLCANO RIDGE –
THREEPOINT CREEK LOOP

This long, loop trip includes Volcano Ridge trail, Threepoint Creek trail, North Fork trail and the Gorge Creek Truck Trail (gravel road).

VOLCANO RIDGE - Cycle Volcano Ridge trail (#65) over Volcano Ridge to the junction with Volcano Creek trail. The Volcano Ridge trail continues north, dipping into two small creek valleys. It is a good dirt road through pine forest that descends to Threepoint Creek, then follows the north side of the creek to the junction of Threepoint Creek trail and Wildhorse trail. This is the start of the spectacular Threepoint Creek Gorge with its black shale walls streaked with sheep trails.

The THREEPOINT CREEK trail is a former road which has been downgraded to smooth trail. Motorized trail bikes occasionally stray out of the McLean Creek Off-Highway Vehicle Zone onto this trail.

The NORTH FORK trail is the least enjoyable part of the trip. Tree roots and soil eroded by cattle make for 5 km of rough cycling. An alternate route, without crossing Threepoint Creek, is to continue down Threepoint Creek to the Gorge Creek Truck Trail. This option adds 5 km and a considerable elevation gain.

GORGE CREEK TRUCK TRAIL - Those of you with true grit can cycle back on Link Creek trail but the rest of us will stick to the Gorge Creek road. This winding gravel road follows the meadows along Link Creek and Ware Creek back to Gorge Creek trailhead.

RATING
Tough
DISTANCE
41.3 km round trip
TIME
6 - 7 hours round trip
ELEVATION GAIN
710 m (2350 ft)
MAPS
82 J/10 Mount Rae
82 J/15 Bragg Creek

ACCESS
Drive west from Turner Valley along Sheep River Trail (S.R. 546) for 30.5 km to the Gorge Creek Truck Trail (gravel road) located between the Sheep Ranger Station and Gorge Creek. Drive north on this narrow gravel road for 4 km to the Gorge Creek trailhead.

CYCLING OPTION
LINK CREEK trail is an alternative access route to Volcano Ridge. It is a good dirt road snaking up an open ridge but has one very steep section that is difficult to push a bicycle up. Volcano Ridge trail is a better option to start the trip.

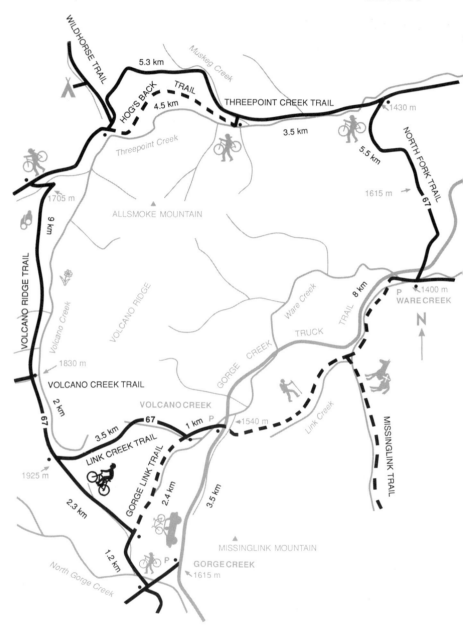

MAP 33

WILDHORSE TRAIL

5.3 km

Muskeg Creek

HOG'S BACK TRAIL

4.5 km

THREEPOINT CREEK TRAIL

3.5 km

1430 m

Threepoint Creek

NORTH FORK TRAIL

5.5 km

67

1705 m

1615 m

ALLSMOKE MOUNTAIN

VOLCANO RIDGE TRAIL

9 km

Volcano Creek

VOLCANO RIDGE

Ware Creek

8 km

TRUCK

P 1400 m

WARE CREEK

N

1830 m

GORGE CREEK

VOLCANO CREEK TRAIL

2 km

VOLCANO CREEK

67

Link Creek

MISSINGLINK TRAIL

67

3.5 km

1 km

P

1540 m

LINK CREEK TRAIL

1925 m

GORGE LINK TRAIL

2.4 km

3.5 km

2.3 km

1.2 km

P

MISSINGLINK MOUNTAIN

GORGE CREEK

1615 m

North Gorge Creek

68 MAP 34
JUNCTION MOUNTAIN FIRE LOOKOUT ROAD

Junction Mountain Fire Lookout Road goes from Indian Oils trailhead to Junction Fire Lookout perched on the north-east ridge of Junction Mountain. The trail is signed as Sheep trail, Green Mountain and Junction Mountain trails, but it is really one continuous dirt road. Although a very enjoyable trail, parts of the road are steep and rocky and you can expect to walk 3 or 4 km out of 10.1 km on the way up.

The trail crosses the Sheep River on a log bridge high above the water. Tiger Jaws Fall lies upstream and there is a colourful shale canyon downstream. Grind your gears up a short, steep hill that climbs out of the river valley. The road levels off and drops down to Dyson Creek. Large swaths of pine and poplar have been cut along the road to improve grazing for cattle. Dyson Falls can be found downstream from the shallow ford of Dyson Creek. A platform in the meadow that looks like a lifeguards' chair was used by University of Calgary researchers for observing the behaviour of the Columbian ground squirrels. Fill your water bottles at Dyson Creek - it may be the last water on the trail.

The next 6.8 km of trail climbs steadily toward the lookout. Stay right at the fork where Green Mountain trail meets Junction Mountain trail. Cattle have left their impressions on the lower parts of the trail near the fork. At 6.0 km the trail becomes steep and covered in boulders - don't despair, it soon becomes smooth again. At 6.6 km the trail emerges out of the pines onto the ridge of Junction Mountain and your efforts are rewarded by the view. Push and peddle up the last 4 km along this alpine ridge where marmots whistle at your passing. You may want to hide your bike and walk the last kilometre of road which is very rocky.

Calgary can be seen from the lookout on a clear day. Blue Ridge lies to the east, Bluerock Mountain to the north-west, Mount Rae pokes its head above the Highwood Range and the grey wall of Junction

RATING
Terrific
DISTANCE
10.1 km to fire lookout
TIME
5 - 8 hours round trip
ELEVATION GAIN
770 m (2500 ft)
MAP
82 J/10 Mount Rae

ACCESS
Park at Indian Oils trailhead on the south side of Sheep River Trail (S.R. 546), 35 km west of Turner Valley.

Mountain stands to the south-west. The remains of a small forest fire which occurred in January of 1986 can be seen to the north. Accidentally ignited by workers clearing trees for grazing improvement, it spread quickly through pines dried out by unusually warm weather.

The first 4 km of the return ride is steep and bumpy.

CYCLING OPTION
GREEN MOUNTAIN TRAIL
This good dirt road could be used as a connection from Dyson Creek to the Phone Line and Mount McNabb trails (#69). It has level grades through pine forest. For more information on these trails consult the Kananaskis Country Trail Guide

MAP 34

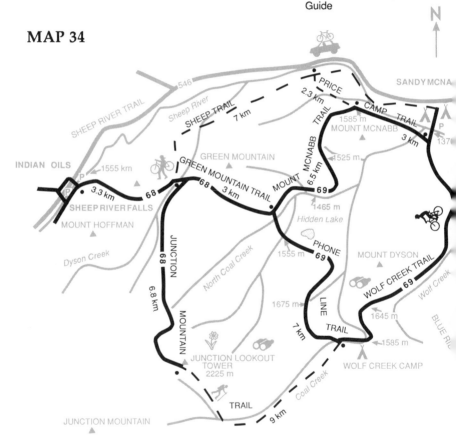

69 MAP 34
WOLF CREEK –
COAL CREEK LOOP

This loop trip follows Wolf Creek trail, Phone Line trail, Mount McNabb trail, and Price Camp trail. It offers mostly smooth cycling on dirt trail and exploration roads, although you can expect parts of the trail to get messed up by cattle during wet conditions. Fortunately, all the trails are marked with signs and red diamonds or it could get hopelessly confusing. This is lower foothills country with no major elevation gain but lots of small hills as the trail cuts across the drainages. Take lots of water if you are shy about sharing a creek with cattle.

WOLF CREEK - Start by fording the Sheep River. High water may make this crossing difficult until late June. Wolf Creek trail has easier cycling than the other trails. A smooth dirt road rises gently through mixed forest to the meadows along the creek, then grows faint as it climbs through pine forest between Mount Dyson and Blue Ridge. The pass between Wolf Creek and Coal Creek is definitely the highlight of the trip. The gentle terrain gives no forewarning of the spectacular black shale canyon of Coal Creek. The meadow at the pass also allows a clear view of Blue Ridge to the south and Junction Lookout to the west. The trail makes a bumpy descent through meadows to Wolf Creek backcountry campground and crosses Coal Creek three times.

PHONE LINE trail offers a narrow winding ride on a single track through pine forest. It is mostly smooth trail covered with pine needles although there are some low wet spots where you will have to walk the bike. The steep banks on North Coal Creek may require you to carry the bike.

The trail follows the route of a "fence-wire" phone line, part of the old Alberta Forest Service telephone line built in the 1920's from Coleman to Nordegg. The wire was strung on tripods and from insulators hung from trees. When this primitive phone service was replaced by radios in the 1950's, the wires were removed because they were a hazard to big game animals and cattle.

RATING
Tough
DISTANCE
27.5 km loop
TIME
4 - 6 hours round trip
ELEVATION GAIN
515 m (1690 ft)
MAP
82 J/10 Mount Rae

ACCESS
The Wolf Creek trail starts at Sandy McNabb Recreation Area 21 km west of Turner Valley on Sheep River Trail (S.R. 546). The trailhead can be found in the equestrian parking lot, the first turn to the left as you enter the recreation area. You might prefer to pick up the trail where it crosses the Sheep River. Drive to the bottom of the hill and look for the red diamonds on trees that mark the trail.

MOUNT MCNABB trail follows a dirt road along the north side of North Coal Creek. It offers some of the prettiest meadows and aspen groves in the area, but has the annoying habit of crossing the creek too many times. The trail veers north and follows a cow path through a meadow and over a low pass. The north side of the pass has a narrow, bumpy, steep and downright devious trail where your bullmoose bars will graze the poplars.

PRICE CAMP - The only redeeming feature of Price Camp trail is that it is short. It is heavily travelled by cattle and crossed with poplar roots. The trail is named after Price, a Turner Valley resident who operated a saw mill here in the early 1900's.

"Where do I go now?" Colynn Kerr above Coal Creek Canyon.

70 MAP 32 & 35
SHEEP TRAIL

The Sheep trail is a good gravel road with some rough spots. An old bridge over the Sheep River at the 3 km point has been improved to make for an easy crossing. Numerous shallow stream crossings, especially on the upper section north of Burns Creek, ensure that your feet will be wet for most of the trip.

The early part of the trip is dominated by spectacular views of Gibraltar Mountain. Its north face was the site of the first extended aid climb in the Canadian Rockies. The climbers were on the face for 8 1/2 days and many pitches were overhanging for their entire length.

At the junction with the Mist Creek trail (#71) you'll discover a pile of coal and a corral, remnants of development by the P. Burns Coal Mines Company.

The pass between the Sheep and Elbow rivers presents an austere but hauntingly beautiful landscape composed of burned over larch and fir forest. The larches on the hillsides indicate you are near to treeline. It is unusual to encounter a good gravel road in such a high area.

RATING
Tough
DISTANCE
22 km to Elbow River
TIME
5 - 8 hours round trip
ELEVATION GAIN
515 m (1690 ft)
MAPS
82 J/10 Mount Rae

ACCESS
From Turner Valley drive, 38 km up Sheep River Trail (S.R. 546) to the Junction Creek picnic area at the end of the road. The trail starts as a gated road at the west end of the picnic area.

CYCLING OPTION
BURNS CREEK
Three kilometres north of the Mist Creek trail, a seismic road leaves the west side of the Sheep trail. It follows the north shore of Burns Creek for 5.5 km almost to the base of a 400 m-high waterfall cascading over a headwall. This makes an excellent destination for a cycling trip up the Sheep River. Burns Lake lies beyond, but requires a steep climb past the waterfall to reach its shores.

Sheryle Elliot fording the Sheep River.
"Keeping the bearings dry".

MAP 35

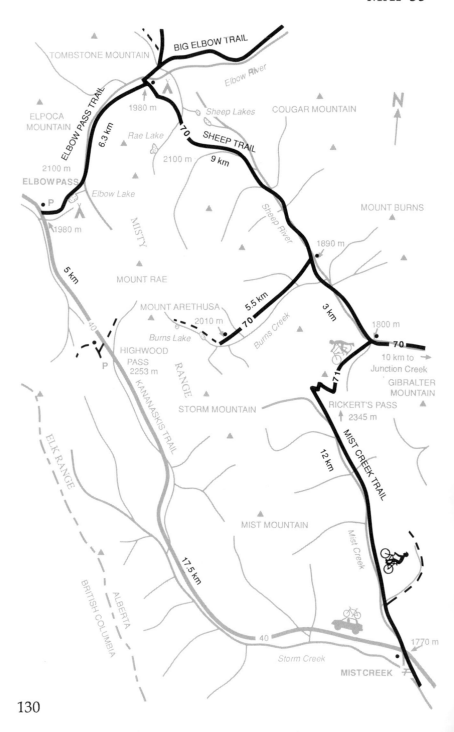

71 MAP 35
AROUND THE MISTY RANGE

The loop consists of Kananaskis Trail (Hwy. 40), Elbow Pass trail (#61), Sheep trail (#70) and Mist Creek trail back to Mist Creek trailhead. This is a long and arduous trip not to be taken lightly. The route circumnavigates the Misty Range, a range of 3000 m peaks deeply carved with glacial cirques, and is a feast for the eyes and the imagination. Riding the entire loop in one day is only suitable for seasoned mountain bikers. You must get an early start and have clear dry weather. Rickert's Pass is snowed in until mid June.

From Mist Creek trailhead, cycle 22.5 km on the wide paved shoulders of Kananaskis Trail (Hwy. 40) over Highwood Pass, the highest drivable pass in Canada (2206.3 m), to Elbow Pass trailhead. Cycle the trail to Elbow Lake (#61) and follow down the Elbow River to Sheep trail (#70). The pass between the Sheep and Elbow Rivers is good riding on gravel road through open, burned over larch and fir forest. The lower part of the Sheep trail has some rough spots and numerous stream crossings.

MIST CREEK - At the junction with the Mist Creek trail there is a pile of coal and a corral, remnants of development by the P. Burns Coal Mines Company. The difficult part of the loop trip is the steep push up the Mist Creek trail to Rickert's Pass (545 m in 2.5 km). A road winds uphill to an excavation in the hillside. A steep trail continues through pine forest to alpine meadows where switchbacks lead to the pass. The hard work on the way up is rewarded with yet another striking view of the Misty Range and the prospect of a long downhill ride.

On the west side of the pass the trail quickly drops into the forest. Most of this trail is rideable in the downhill mode but you would have to push if you were travelling up the trail. The roots make for bumpy riding on this forest trail. The trail joins a dirt road for the last kilometre back to Mist Creek trailhead.

RATING
Terrific - dry weather only
DISTANCE
53 km round trip
TIME
7 - 12 hours hard riding
ELEVATION GAIN
1270 m (4070 ft)
MAPS
82 J/10 Mount Rae
82 J/11 Kananaskis Lakes

ACCESS
The Mist Creek trailhead, 17.5 km south of Highwood Pass on Kananaskis Trail (Hwy. 40) is a good place to start this loop trip.

72 MAP 36
LANTERN CREEK
TO MIST CREEK

This short, easy trail provides a diversion through the pine forests and ponds along the Highwood River.

From Lantern Creek picnic area cycle 0.5 km north on Kananaskis Trail (Hwy. 40) to an obscure road to the west blocked by a large rock marked with a large letter M. The vegetated gravel surface offers easy cycling. At 1.6 km the road passes the Trout Ponds, a series of beaver ponds civilized with paths and picnic tables. At 2.2 km the trail crosses a gravel pit with a paved road. A little farther on cycle over a tank trap which blocks the trail continuing north to Mist Creek picnic area.

The wide paved shoulders of Kananaskis Trail provide an easy return trip.

CAUTION: The gravel pit is sometimes used as a shooting range, especially in August and September as hunting season approaches.

RATING
Tender
DISTANCE
7.2 km round trip
TIME
1 hour round trip
ELEVATION GAIN
30 m (100 ft)
MAPS
82 J/7 Mount Head
82 J/10 Mount Rae

ACCESS
Park at Lantern Creek picnic area on Kananaskis Trail (Hwy. 40), 88.2 km south of the Trans-Canada Highway and 17.2 km north of Highwood Junction.

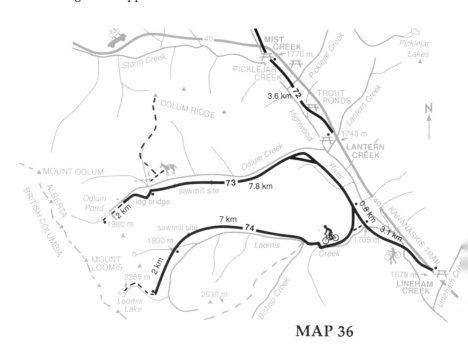

MAP 36

132

73 MAP 36
ODLUM POND

This road up Odlum Creek ends near Odlum Pond, a small lake in a cirque. It provides some of the easiest and most pleasant cycling in the Highwood Valley along a smooth gravel surface that is partly vegetated.

Highwood River must be forded 1.6 km from Lineham Creek picnic area. The ford is axle deep, 30 m wide and slow flowing in midsummer but difficult to cross in the spring. Take the right fork after the shallow Loomis Creek crossing. The left fork goes up Loomis Creek while the much better right fork follows a bench that parallels the Highwood River. Grouseberries carpet the pine forest and strawberries line the edges of the road. The road climbs steadily but gently up Odlum Creek, breaching the low mountains west of the Highwood River.

The upper Odlum Valley is covered by spruce and fir forest that bears the scars of logging and fire. The road crosses two sawmill sites where the road has been obliterated for short stretches, then deteriorates to a smooth dirt road and crosses Odlum Creek on a old log bridge. Don't follow the road across the bridge. Find the rough logging road on the south side of the creek which leads to two beaver ponds surrounded by drowned trees. A game trail continues to Odlum Pond, a shallow lake in a meadow surrounded by the walls of a cirque in the Elk Range. Odlum Creek tumbles down for over 100 m in a spectacular waterfall.

The ride back is smooth and fast but watch out for washed-out culverts and cyclists stopping to graze on strawberries.

RATING
Tender
DISTANCE
13.7 km one way
TIME
4 - 5 hours return
ELEVATION GAIN
305 m (1000 ft)
MAP
82 J/7 Mount Head

ACCESS
Park at Lineham Creek picnic area on Kananaskis Trail (Hwy. 40), 93.4 km south of the Trans-Canada Highway and 12.0 km north of Highwood Junction. From the parking lot at Lineham Creek, cycle 200 m north on Kananaskis Trail (Hwy. 40) to the trailhead which is a gated road on the west side of the highway.

HIKING OPTION
ODLUM RIDGE - From the log bridge on Odlum Creek an interesting option is to bushwhack to the windswept meadows on Odlum Ridge. For more information on these trails consult the Kananaskis Country Trail Guide

LOOMIS CREEK & LAKE

The trail follows a logging road up Loomis Creek to Loomis Lake, a high alpine lake in the south end of the Elk Range. The last kilometre is a steep hike without a trail.

Follow the Odlum Creek trail from Lineham Creek picnic area. Ford the Highwood River and cross Loomis Creek 3.1 km from the trailhead. Cycle 800 m further on the Odlum Creek road to the junction with the Loomis Creek logging road.

The Loomis Creek road is a good dirt road which climbs gently through a gap in the range of low mountains west of the Highwood River. After four stream crossings in a row, the Bishop Creek logging road branches to the south. The valley now opens up and provides pleasant cycling through open mixed forest and meadows. Past the sawmill site the road gradually deteriorates and becomes more vegetated. Avoid the lower roads which drop to the creek.

Leave the bikes at the end of the road and bush-whack up the north side of Loomis Creek. It is a short but steep hike up meadows and benches to the lake, nestled in a cirque below an unnamed peak. The lake is dammed by a wall of terminal moraine.

RATING
Tough
DISTANCE
13 km to Loomis Lake
TIME
4 - 6 hours return
ELEVATION GAIN
215 m (700 ft) biking
395 m (1300 ft) hiking
MAP
82 J/7 Mount Head

ACCESS
Park at Lineham Creek picnic area on Kananaskis Trail (Hwy. 40). Via Odlum Pond trail (#72) at the 3.9 km point.

HIKING / CYCLING OPTION
BISHOP CREEK - A bike-hike up the steep Bishop Creek logging road takes you above treeline to a col below Mount Bishop.
For more information on these trails consult the Kananaskis Country Trail Guide

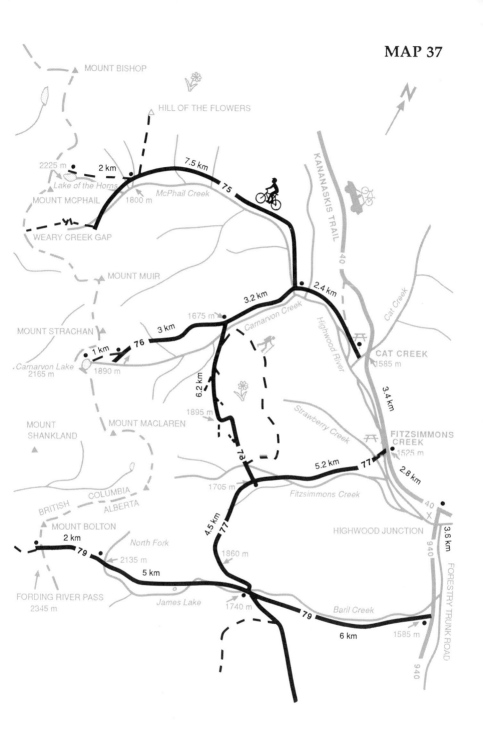

MAP 37

MOUNT BISHOP

HILL OF THE FLOWERS

2225 m

2 km

7.5 km

75

Lake of the Horns

McPhail Creek

MOUNT MCPHAIL

1800 m

74

WEARY CREEK GAP

MOUNT MUIR

KANANASKIS TRAIL

40

2.4 km

3.2 km

Carnarvon Creek

Cat Creek

1675 m

3 km

76

Highwood River

CAT CREEK

1585 m

MOUNT STRACHAN

1 km

Camarvon Lake
2165 m

1890 m

3.4 km

6.2 km

Strawberry Creek

1895 m

MOUNT
SHANKLAND

MOUNT MACLAREN

FITZSIMMONS
CREEK
1525 m

78

5.2 km

77

2.8 km

COLUMBIA

1705 m

Fitzsimmons Creek

40

X

BRITISH

ALBERTA

HIGHWOOD JUNCTION

940

3.6 km

MOUNT BOLTON

2 km

79

4.5 km

77

North Fork

2135 m

1860 m

5 km

FORDING RIVER PASS
2345 m

James Lake

1740 m

79

Baril Creek

6 km

1585 m

940

FORESTRY TRUNK ROAD

135

MCPHAIL CREEK
TO LAKE OF THE HORNS

A good dirt logging road provides easy cycling and quick access to the start of the Lake of the Horns hiking trail. Weary Creek Gap and the Hill of the Flowers are both excellent optional hikes.

Initially, the road leads you northwards from the trailhead through meadows along the river where cattle are often grazing. In August the ford of the Highwood River is knee deep and 20 m-wide but the current is slow.

Past the river, the fork on the right takes you along a bench high above McPhail Creek. Watch for a salt lick on the north side of the road. It is a large muddy depression with numerous game trails radiating out from it through the meadows and open pine forest. This area was burned over in 1936 by a huge fire that crept over the pass from the Elk River Valley.

There are several forks in the road but they all return to the main route which is fairly obvious. The road fades out at the head of the valley near the trailheads for several interesting destinations.

Lake of the Horns trail is a narrow hiking trail starting from the north side of the road between two small creeks. It climbs steeply through several cliff bands on the lower slopes of Mount McPhail but the lake is well worth the effort and provides a refreshing swim on a sunny day.

RATING
Tough
DISTANCE
9.9 km cycle
2 km hike
TIME
6-7 hours return
ELEVATION GAIN
215 m (700 ft) cycling
425 m (1,400 ft) hiking
MAPS
82 J/7 Mount Head

ACCESS
Park at Cat Creek day use area on the west side of Kananaskis Trail (Hwy. 40), 99.8 km south of the Trans-Canada Highway and 5.6 km north of Highwood Junction. The trail starts at a gated roas on the north side of the picnic area.

HIKING OPTIONS
WEARY CREEK GAP
The headwall below Weary Creek Gap looks intimidating but there is an easy elk trail that switchbacks up through the cliff bands.
THE HILL OF THE FLOWERS
To gain the summit you must bushwhack up the south ridge of this pyramid shaped hill which stands apart from the main range.
For more information on these trails consult the Kananaskis Country Trail Guide

CARNARVON CREEK

This logging road up Carnarvon Creek offers good cycling and excellent scenery. This trail is best in summer when the ford on the Highwood River is easier and the weather is warm enough to make a swim in Carnarvon lake bearable. The lake is a popular fishing spot for cutthroat trout.

From the Cat Creek picnic area cycle north along the river for 2 km to the wide ford of the Highwood River. Stay left at the major junction 300 m past the ford and cross McPhail Creek. Follow the logging road on the north side of Carnarvon Creek.

Stay right at the junction with the Strawberry Hills logging road (#78). The many forks in the road can be confusing but one fork usually looks much more travelled than another and pointers and cairns left by others lead the way. There a impressive view of the High Rock Range near the end of the road.

The ride back down the road is most enjoyable.

RATING
Tough
DISTANCE
9.6 km to Carnarvon Lake
TIME
4-6 hours round trip
ELEVATION GAIN
300 m (1000 ft) cycling
275 m (900 ft) hiking to lake
MAPS
82 J/7 Mount Head

ACCESS
Park at Cat Creek day use area on the west side of Kananaskis Trail (Hwy. 40), 99.8 km south of the Trans-Canada Highway and 5.6 km north of Highwood Junction. Via McPhail Creek trail (#75).

HIKING OPTION
CARNARVON LAKE
Don't follow the road all the way to the scree slope below the headwall. Look for a trail to the north that traverses the scree slope to a waterfall. A short, exposed, moderately difficult scramble over rock bands beside the waterfall leads to the colourful little lake surrounded by meadows and rock walls.
For more information on these trails consult the Kananaskis Country Trail Guide

Jo-Ann Draper on Carnarvon Lake trail
Last descent before steep hike to Carnarvon Lake.

FITZSIMMONS CREEK LOOP

This loop trip along mostly good logging roads includes the Fitzsimmons Creek trail, Baril Creek trail (#79), the Forestry Trunk Road (S.R. 940) and Kananaskis Trail (Hwy. 40).

FITZSIMMONS CREEK - From Fitzsimmons Creek picnic area, ford the Highwood River which is usually less than axle deep in July and August to a dirt road leading through meadows to the edge of the river valley. A vegetated dirt logging road rises steadily up the north side of Fitzsimmons Creek through open lodgepole pine and trembling aspen forest. The massive wall of Mount Armstrong dominates the view to the west. Holy Cross Mountain and Mount Head in the Highwood Range come into view to the east. The junction with Strawberry Hills trail (#78) is about 0.5 km past the crossing of the north fork of Fitzsimmons Creek, a minor creek crossing.

Signs of past logging are more obvious near the top of the pass where several old roads branch off the main route. Mount Baril rises across the Baril Creek Valley.

BARIL CREEK - It is a good ride down to Baril Creek trail (#79) on a slightly bumpy logging road. Baril Creek is bridged with two large logs. From the junction with trail #81, the Baril Creek trail is mostly a downhill ride on a rough dirt logging road.

The Forestry Trunk Road (gravel), and Kananaskis Trail (Hwy. 40), a paved road with wide shoulders, allow you to complete the journey back to Fitzsimmons Creek picnic area.

RATING
Tough
DISTANCE
22.1 km
TIME
3 - 5 hours round trip
ELEVATION GAIN
335 m (1100 ft)
MAP
82 J/7 Mount Head

ACCESS
The trail starts at Fitzsimmons Creek picnic area on the west side of Kananaskis Trail (Hwy. 40), 2.8 km north of Highwood Junction and 102.6 km south of the Trans-Canada Highway.

78 MAP 37
STRAWBERRY HILLS

The Strawberry Hills trail is an old logging road providing a useful link between Carnarvon Creek (#76) and Fitzsimmons Creek (#77) and has the potential for a loop trip of 20.4 km along these two creeks and Kananaskis Trail (Hwy. 40).

The north end of the road is much easier to find. There is a major fork in the road up Carnarvon Creek 3.2 km from the crossing of McPhail Creek. The left fork crosses Carnarvon Creek in 400 m. Several grey log loading ramps remain standing on the south side of the creek.

It is pleasant open country that has been logged and burnt and has regrown in pine and aspen. There are good views of the pyramid peak of Mount Strachan and the massive wall of Mount Armstrong. Unfortunately, the dirt road is usually roughened by the hooves of numerous elk and cattle and makes for bumpy cycling. Several logging roads branch off and cause confusion in route finding - if in doubt choose the more travelled and obvious fork in the road. Many of the branching roads rejoin again. The road makes a T-junction with the Fitzsimmons Creek road 0.5 km south of the crossing of the north fork of Fitzsimmons Creek.

RATING
Tough - dry weather only
DISTANCE
6.2 km
TIME
1 - 2 hours
ELEVATION GAIN
220 m (720 ft) from Carnarvon Creek
190 m (620 ft) from Fitzsimmons Creek
MAP
82 J/7 Mount Head

NORTH ACCESS
Via Carnarvon Creek trail (#76) at 5.6 km point.

SOUTH ACCESS
Via Fitzsimmons Creek trail (#77) at 5.2 km point.

Strawberry patrol in the Strawberry Hills.
From left to right: Jacquie, Rundy, Claudia, Jo-Ann, Nancy, Ed, Kathy

79 MAP 37
BARIL CREEK
TO FORDING RIVER PASS

The Baril Creek trail follows a dirt logging and seismic road up Baril Creek to Fording River Pass in the High Rock Range which is an important link in the Great Divide Trail. The trip should be saved for dry weather since the lower part of the road can be quite muddy. The road becomes smoother later in the summer as it dries and the elk and cattle tracks level out.

The first 6 km of road climbs steadily through pine and spruce forest bearing the signs of logging and fire. A log bridge crosses Baril Creek near the junction with the Fitzsimmons Creek trail.

One kilometre further west you pass an old sawmill site, then descend a steep hill and cross the creek twice. The road is rocky in places and the route can be confusing since the seismic road intermingles with the Great Divide Trail. Watch out for James Lake, a lovely pond between the road and the trail.

At some point you will want to hide your bikes and hike the rest of the way to the pass as the road gets steeper. The seismic road crosses the north fork of Baril Creek and rises straight up a very steep hill. There is a good campsite at the base of the hill by the creek.

The rolling, open meadows on Fording River Pass are an invitation to explore. The well-formed cirques on Mount Cornwall form a spectacular backdrop to the small alpine lakes. It is an easy scramble up Mount Bolton.

The ride out along Baril Creek is fast and enjoyable east of the sawmill site.

RATING
Tough - dry weather only
DISTANCE
13 km to Fording River Pass
TIME
6 - 7 hours round trip
ELEVATION GAIN
550 m (1800 ft) bicycling
210 m (700 ft) hiking
MAP
82 J/7 Mount Head

ACCESS
The best access is from a gravel pit on the west side of the Forestry Trunk Road (S.R. 940) 0.5 km south of Baril Creek and 3.6 km south of Highwood Junction.

CYCLING OPTION
FORDING RIVER PASS TO ELK RIVER ROAD - 22 km
The seismic road that crosses Fording River Pass continues down the west side of the pass where it forks into two roads that follow Fording River and Aldridge Creek. The Fording River road is the better road. It eventually swings west and joins the gravel road along the Elk River near Britt Creek. The lower part of this road is also the access road for the Fording Fire Lookout in the Greenhills Range.
This opens up possibilities for more ambitious trips involving Elk Pass (#49) to the north and North Fork Pass (#96) to the south.

80 MAP 38
CATARACT - RYE RIDGE - ETHERINGTON LOOP

The logging roads up Cataract and Etherington creeks offer easy cycling while the trail joining them over Rye Ridge is difficult due to its narrow width, exposed roots and the push up onto the ridge.

The CATARACT CREEK road (#88) is a smooth, gravel road that was recently upgraded because of logging activity in the Lost Creek Valley to the south.

RYE RIDGE - The trail over Rye Ridge is identified as the "Cataract Loop" and the "Etherington" trails on the snowmobile trail signs. The Cataract Loop trail is much rougher than the gravel road along Cataract and Lost creeks. Scraped bare to improve it as a snowmobile trail, it's been left with a muddy surface that is extremely sticky when wet. The trail surface will improve as it becomes more vegetated. As the trail climbs toward Rye Ridge, the Great Divide Trail marked with red blazes provides a better route than the bulldozed snowmobile trails. Push uphill through pine forest to the open windswept meadow on Rye Ridge. You will be rewarded by magnificent views of Mount Etherington and Baril Peak in the High Rock Range. Ride the ridge as it slopes downward toward Etherington Creek. More walking is required on the narrow, switchbacking trail that descends to Etherington Creek.

ETHERINGTON CREEK - The relatively smooth, fast riding on the dirt surface of the Etherington Creek road is a relief. The upper part of the road is sometimes roughened by cattle and elk but it gets smoother later in the summer. The lower part of the road is gravel and there are several shallow creek crossings. Watch out for horses.

Return to the trailhead on the gravel surface of the Forestry Trunk Road (S.R. 940).

RATING
Terrific - dry weather only
DISTANCE
31.5 km round trip
TIME
5 - 8 hours round trip
ELEVATION GAIN
555 m (1800 ft)
MAP
82 J/7 Mount Head

ACCESS
The trailhead lies at the junction of the Forestry Trunk Road (S.R. 940) and the Raspberry Fire Lookout Road, 11.6 km south of Highwood Junction. Park at the Raspberry Lookout road or 2 km further south at the Cataract Creek Recreation Area.

CYCLING OPTION
A loop trip of 16.4 km can be cycled using the Etherington Creek trail, Baril Loop (#81), Baril Creek trail (#79) and the Forestry Trunk Road.

81 MAP 38
BARIL LOOP

Baril Loop is part of the Cataract Creek snow-mobile trail system which is marked with orange squares. The west part of the loop is a rough, uncom-pacted road that is not enjoyable cycling. The east part of the loop, which is an old logging road connect-ing Etherington and Baril Creeks, crosses a low pass providing good views of Raspberry Fire Lookout, Baril Peak, Mount Head and Mist Mountain. The south part of the road is largely dirt which is muddy in the spring, while the north part has more gravel.

RATING
Tough - dry weather only
DISTANCE
4.0 km
TIME
1 hour
ELEVATION GAIN
160 m (525 ft) from Ethering-ton Creek
125 m (410 ft) from Baril Creek
MAP
82 J/7 Mount Head

NORTH ACCESS
Via Baril Creek (#79).

SOUTH ACCESS
Via Etherington Creek (#80).

MAP 38

82 MAP 38
RASPBERRY PASS

Raspberry Pass trail is part of the Cataract Creek snowmobile trail system which is marked by orange squares. It is of little interest for its own sake but is a useful connection between Etherington Creek and Cataract Creek and forms part of the Low Divide trail (#90). The north end starts out as a good, gravel logging road but deteriorates to a rough uncompacted snowmobile trail with wet and marshy spots. It is best to ride it from north to south so that elevation is gained on the smoother gravel road. Avoid this trail in wet weather.

RATING
Tough - dry weather only
DISTANCE
6.1 km
TIME
2 -3 hours
ELEVATION GAIN
185 m (600 ft) from Etherington Creek
215 m (700 ft) from Cataract Creek
MAP
82 J/7 Mount Head

NORTH ACCESS
Via Etherington Creek (#80)

SOUTH ACCESS
Via Cataract Creek (#88)

83 MAP 39
CATARACT CREEK TO UPPER FALLS

If you are looking for a quick ride after dinner then take off your panniers and put your wet shoes back on. The narrow parts of the trail involve some technical maneuvering and log jumping and there is one axle-deep ford.

The trip starts on a bumpy road crossing the meadow on the cobble flats south of Cataract campground. Mount Burke in the east can look quite dramatic in the evening sun. The road crosses the creek after 2.5 km then appears to dead end in the creek. Don't give up. Thrash through the willows for a few metres to pick up the single track. One kilometre of narrow and winding trail leads to a cliff overlooking Upper Cataract Falls which plunges over a limestone cap rock into a deep pool in a canyon.

The trail continues for 10 km down Cataract Creek to Highwood Trail (S.R. 541). However, it is an undeveloped route requiring some bushwhacking and is no place for a bicycle.

RATING
Tough
DISTANCE
3.5 km to falls
TIME
1 hour return
ELEVATION LOSS
30 m (100 ft)
MAP
82 J/7 Mount Head

ACCESS
From Highwood Junction, drive 13.6 km south on the Forestry Trunk Road (S.R. 940) to Cataract Creek Recreation Area. The trail head is a gated road next to campsite #27.

143

84 MAP 39
SALTER CREEK
TO WILLOW CREEK

This trip is highly recommended; the cycling is mostly easy going on old roads and the Eastern Slopes scenery is at its best. Take water because the creeks may be dry by midsummer. Because of the long distance, the low elevation gain and smooth cycling, this route makes a good overnight trip.

SALTER CREEK - The lower part of the trail along Salter Creek is rocky riding but the trail becomes smoother in the meadows near Salter Pass. The upper trail passes through a long meadow nestled between Mount Burke and Plateau Mountain. From the top of Salter Pass there are impressive views of Sentinel Peak and Sentinel Pass.

PEKISKO CREEK AND WILLOW CREEK - The roads down Pekisko Creek and Willow Creek offer smooth and pleasant cycling. The Pekisko Creek road travels through meadows and poplar and pine forest. The junction with the Willow Creek trails can be a little confusing - follow the snowmobile signs along Willow Creek. The road passes through pasture land with lots of gates to open and close and cattle to entertain.

The return trip is a 34 km ride on good gravel roads. Johnson Creek Trail (S.R. 532) provides a very scenic and often windy trip over the pass under Hailstone Butte, while the Forestry Trunk Road (S.R. 940) offers a good downhill ride from Wilkinson Summit back to Cataract Creek.

RATING
Tough
DISTANCE
27 km to Indian Graves campground
71 km round trip
TIME
4 - 6 hours to Indian Graves campground
ELEVATION GAIN
315 m (1030 ft) to Indian Graves campground
980 m (3215 ft) round trip
MAPS
82 J/7 Mount Head
82 J/8 Stimson Creek
82 J/1 Langford Creek
82 J/2 Fording River

ACCESS
From Highwood Junction, drive 13 km south along the Forestry Trunk Road (S.R. 940) to Cataract Creek Recreation Area. Salter Creek crosses the campground entrance road. You can start on either side of Salter Creek but the south side is better.

144

MAP 39

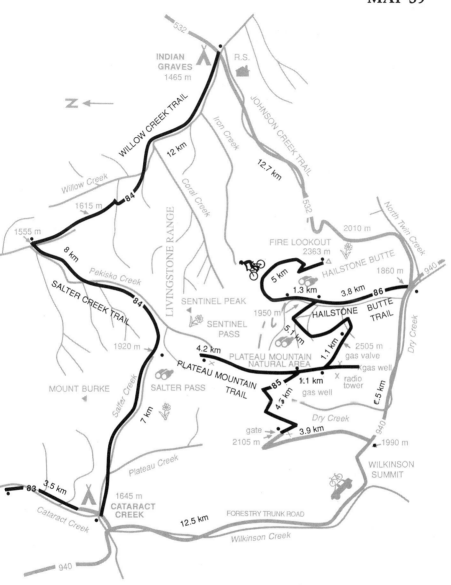

INDIAN GRAVES
1465 m

532

R.S.

WILLOW CREEK TRAIL

12 km

JOHNSON CREEK TRAIL

12.7 km

Iron Creek

Coral Creek

Willow Creek

1615 m

84

1555 m

8 km

Pekisko Creek

84

LIVINGSTONE RANGE

SALTER CREEK TRAIL

SENTINEL PEAK

SENTINEL PASS

1920 m

4.2 km

MOUNT BURKE

Salter Creek

SALTER PASS

7 km

PLATEAU MOUNTAIN TRAIL

PLATEAU MOUNTAIN NATURAL AREA

1950 m

5.1 km

1.1 km

85

2505 m
gas valve

1.1 km

gas well

4 km
gas well

X radio tower

FIRE LOOKOUT
2363 m

5 km

1.3 km

3.8 km

HAILSTONE BUTTE

86

HAILSTONE BUTTE TRAIL

1860 m

2010 m

North Twin Creek

940

Dry Creek

5.5 km

940

gate
2105 m

3.9 km

Dry Creek

1990 m

WILKINSON SUMMIT

Plateau Creek

83

3.5 km

Cataract Creek

1645 m
CATARACT CREEK

12.5 km

FORESTRY TRUNK ROAD

Wilkinson Creek

940

N ←

85 MAP 39
PLATEAU MOUNTAIN

This is probably the only restricted access road in the Rockies that provides an easy cycle trip to the top of a mountain. It is best to pick a calm day to cycle this peak. Bring your own water.

The mountain is unique in that it was a nunatak, or non-glaciated peak during the last glaciation. Ten thousand years ago when the surrounding valleys and peaks were covered in ice, the flat top of Plateau Mountain remained ice free. This allowed the development of patterned ground, a periglacial feature consisting of polygons of rock. Freeze thaw action tends to separate rocks from the smaller particles of soil. Thousands of years of this action, uninterrupted by the scouring of glaciers, results in a honeycomb of rocks over the surface of the ground. The mountain provided a rare, ice free habitat for plants and animals during glaciation.

Cycle up the wide, gravel road that rises in huge switchbacks through the alpine meadow. The culverts provide shelter for porcupines and golden mantled ground squirrels. A herd of Rocky Mountain sheep frequents the meadows and peregrine and prairie falcons are sometimes seen doing aerial acrobatics in the wind currents. At 4.5 km the road forks. The south fork leads to the flat summit and a radio tower powered by a wind generator.

The north fork drops gently for 4.2 km through the plateau to an abandoned drilling platform. There are excellent examples of patterned ground along the way with buttercups, alpine forget-me-nots and moss campion growing among the lichen-covered rocks. A plaque at the end of the road introduces you to another unique feature of Plateau Mountain, the ice caves. The caves are now gated to preserve the delicate ice features. Aside from vandalism, the caves were deteriorating from the body heat of visitors which melted the ice. To the west, the High Rock Range rises above the meadow like a row of pyramids stamped out of the same glacial mold.

It is interesting to wonder if the drilling activity and road construction on Plateau Mountain would have been allowed if it were proposed today.

RATING
Tender
DISTANCE
5.6 km
TIME
3 hours return
ELEVATION GAIN
400 m (1310 ft)
MAP
82 J/2 Fording River

ACCESS
From Highwood Junction, drive 26.1 km south on the Forestry Trunk Road (S.R. 940) to Wilkinson Summit, the drainage divide between the Highwood and Livingstone Rivers. The Plateau Mountain road to the north has a massive red gate posted with intimidating warnings about sour gas. The gate is usually open and you can drive a further 3.9 km to a locked gate near tree line.

Allison Husband on Plateau Mountain.
Freezing weather in July.

CYCLING OPTION
TWIN SUMMITS ODYSSEY

For the hardy and adventurous fat tire enthusiast, Plateau Mountain can be combined with Hailstone Butte (#86) and the Forestry Trunk Road (S.R. 940) to make a loop trip of 38.6 km and 1058 vertical metres. On the summit of Plateau Mountain, about 200 m north of the radio tower, a narrow road leads to a drilling platform at the south-east edge of the plateau. A faint line of rocks, possibly the route of a pipeline, descends southwest to a col inhabited by marmots which is one of the most bizarre and dramatic places I have ever walked my bicycle. Rolling alpine meadows drop away into rocky canyons. The line of rocks drops to the north-east below tree line to a gas well in a glacial cirque. A smooth gravel road connects with the Hailstone Butte road. After cycling to the top of Hailstone Butte, let your bike coast your tired body back to the Forestry Trunk Road.

147

86 MAP 39
HAILSTONE BUTTE
FIRE LOOKOUT

This trip offers good roads and a panoramic view from the Hailstone Butte fire lookout which is one of the easier lookouts to cycle to.

The lower 3.8 km is a well-travelled gas well access road with meadows and pipelines and grazing cattle. Stay right at the first two forks. The route to the fire lookout is a rocky, seldom travelled road marked by a broken down green and white gate. It climbs up a steep but rideable valley with cliffs rising at its edge. After a gentle ride past a wet meadow the road begins rising again through huge rolling alpine meadows on the east side of Hailstone Butte. The view keeps getting better as the distinctive shape of Saddle Peak rises above the meadow. Push up the steep switchbacks along dirt road trenched by water erosion. The final stretch to the tower is a moderately steep ride along a rocky ridge. Be sure to say hello to "Tower Tom". My bike was only the second one he had seen at the top of the mountain.

Windy Peak and Saddle Peak, part of the Livingstone Range, can be seen to the south. Beehive Mountain, Gould Dome and The Elevators rise from the High Rock Range to the west. The oil towers of Calgary can been seen to the north north-west beyond the rolling foothills. Nearer at hand the steep and colourful Skene Canyon drops away to the east and Plateau Mountain presents its flat top to the immediate west.

RATING
Tough
DISTANCE
10.1 km one way
TIME
4 hours round trip
ELEVATION GAIN
503 m (1650 ft)
MAP
82 J/1 Langford Creek

ACCESS
From Highwood Junction, drive 32.6 km south on the Forestry Trunk Road (S.R. 940) to the junction with Johnson Creek Trail (S.R. 532). The road to Hailstone Butte is a gated road 50 m north of Johnson Creek Trail (S.R. 532).

CYCLING OPTION
GAS WELL ROADS
The two gas well access roads leading to the east from the main access road each present an unusual sight of gas wells drilled in glacial cirques at the edge of Plateau Mountain.

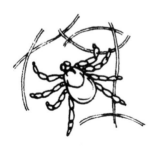

WILKINSON CREEK - CUMMINGS CREEK LOOP

This loop trip follows the Forestry Trunk Road, Cummings Creek snowmobile trail, and the logging roads along Lost Creek and Cataract Creek (#88). It is necessary to push or carry the bike up a short but very steep hill on the Cummings Creek trail.

Cycle south on the Forestry Trunk Road for 8.6 km. This is a good gravel road which follows Wilkinson Creek. Turn west onto a logging road next to a large cutblock. A "no vehicle" sign marks the start of the road. Cycle the road to a bridge over Wilkinson Creek, then take the right fork 100 m further south. The road climbs through a recent cutblock - stay left at the fork in the middle of the cutblock. If you have followed the trail this far, you should find the rest of it quite easily.

The dirt road climbs steadily through pine and spruce forest toward a hill north of Pasque Mountain. Follow the most distinct road. Eventually you will see the orange squares marking the snowmobile trail. The road dips into one more drainage of Wilkinson Creek and then goes straight up a short muddy hill. The choice of route is indicative of the single-minded determination of seismic crews. Your show of brute strength and determination in climbing this hill will be rewarded with a long, steep downhill ride on the other side.

If you came for the view you will be disappointed. However, the hill does have a pleasant pine forest carpeted with grouseberries. The straight seismic line with a smooth shale surface drops steadily to Cummings Creek and eventually emerges out of the trees into a rough clearing. A sign indicates a very rough 1.4 km fork to the west that joins the Lost Creek trail. Do not fall prey to the temptation to continue down Cummings Creek. It has some of the stickiest mud this side of Winnipeg.

A smooth gravel road along Lost Creek and Cataract Creek (#88) leads back to Cataract Creek Recreation Area in 11.3 km.

RATING
Terrific - dry weather only
DISTANCE
29.3 km round trip
TIME
4 - 5 hours round trip
ELEVATION GAIN
430 m (1400 m)
MAPS
82 J/2 Fording River
82 J/7 Mount Head

ACCESS
From Highwood Junction, drive 13.6 km south on the Forestry Trunk Road (S.R. 940) to Cataract Creek Recreation Area. Park at the day use area.

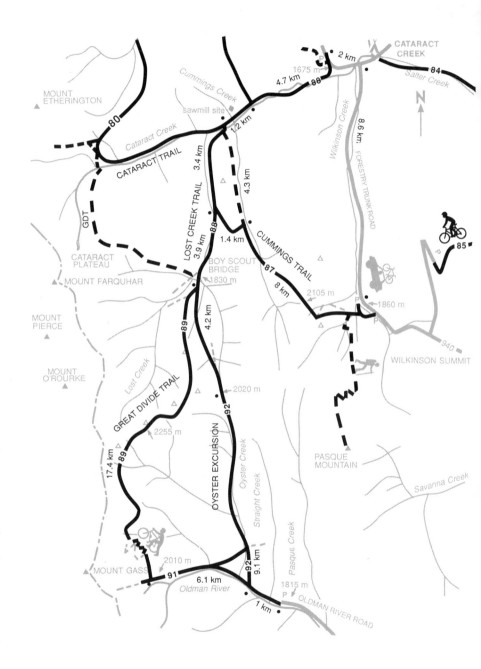

MAP 40

88 MAP 38,40
CATARACT CREEK
TO BOY SCOUT BRIDGE

A recently upgraded logging road follows Cataract Creek and Lost Creek past the Boy Scout bridge to cutblocks in the upper Lost Creek Valley. All creek crossings are bridged. It is an easy, level ride and the starting point for several longer mountain bike trips. This restricted access road is occasionally driven by government workers and logging trucks.

The road along Cataract Creek passes through wide, valley bottom meadows. The creek and its beaver ponds are popular for trout fishing. To the west, Mount Scrimger and Mount Etherington mark the Divide . The large clearing north of Cummings Creek started out as a sawmill site and was later used as a camp for a bear study group.

The obvious gravel road crosses a bridge over Cataract Creek and follows Lost Creek to a fork at 13.2 km. Keep left and cycle through old cutblocks to the Boy Scout Bridge. The bridge was tied together in 1980 by the 153rd Scout Troop but a more substantial road bridge has since been built beside it. The rough logging roads to the south access the Oyster Creek and Great Divide trails. The smooth gravel road along the north bank of Lost Creek leads to cutblocks below Cataract Plateau and Mount Farquhar.

RATING
Tender
DISTANCE
13.2 km to Boy Scout Bridge
TIME
3 - 4 hours round trip
ELEVATION GAIN
155 m (500 ft)
MAPS
82 J/7 Mount Head
82 J/2 Fording River

ACCESS
The trailhead lies at the junction of the Forestry Trunk Road (S.R. 940) and the Raspberry Fire Lookout Road, 11.6 km south of Highwood Junction. Park at the Raspberry Lookout road or 2 km further south at the Cataract Creek Recreation Area.

89 MAP 40
GREAT DIVIDE TRAIL (CATARACT CREEK TO OLDMAN RIVER)

This is a long trip requiring careful planning by strong cyclists. It could be done as a lightweight overnight trip or as an extended day trip using a car shuttle. It is a 76 km drive from Cataract Creek to the end of the Oldman River via the Forestry Trunk Road and the Oldman River Road. The cycling route follows a gravel road to the Boy Scout bridge on Lost Creek (#88). The difficult and rewarding part of the trip is a spectacular section of the Great Divide Trail with a ridge ride along the divide between Lost Creek and the Oldman River.

Cycle the smooth gravel road up Cataract Creek and Lost Creek (#88). At 13.2 km, a dirt road forks left to the Boy Scout Bridge. (The gravel road, the right fork, continues up Lost Creek to a series of cutblocks.) The route over the Boy Scout Bridge is part of a snowmobile route known as the Oyster Excursion (#92) and is marked with orange squares. About 200 m past the Boy Scout bridge, a rough logging road forks to the west (right). You may see red paint blazes that identify this as part of the Great Divide Trail. Another 200 m west on the logging road look carefully for red blazes marking a hiking trail into a mature spruce forest.

The hard part of this trip is now upon you. Push your fat tires for 2 km and 365 vertical metres to the top of a ridge. There are some steep rock steps near the top that may require carrying the bike. This north slope is usually muddy.

The trail improves dramatically after it reaches the sandstone ridge. The meadows and open larch forest provide relief from tree roots. Most of the trail from here to the Galena Miracle Mine is rideable with occasional rough parts. It is a roller coaster with alternate hills to push up and ride down.

There are five distinct hills along this ridge. The first hill has a cairn and a clear view of Cataract Plateau to the north-west which is an important

RATING
Terrific - dry weather only
DISTANCE
37.7 km
TIME
8 - 10 hours
ELEVATION GAIN
700 m (2300 ft)
MAPS
82 J/7 Mount Head
82 J/2 Fording River

NORTH ACCESS
From Highwood Junction, drive 11.6 km south on the Forestry Trunk Road (S.R. 940) to the Raspberry Fire Lookout access road. It lies 2 km north of Cataract Creek Recreation Area.

SOUTH ACCESS
From Highwood Junction drive 48 km south on the Forestry Trunk Road (S.R. 940) to the Oldman River Road. Drive 28 km to the end of the Oldman River Road which ends at a beaver pond near Straight Creek.

summer grazing area for elk. The second hill is surrounded by meadows created by a burn. The third
hill has a spring for the thirsty traveller. The fourth
hill which is above treeline has a shale ridge that
drops away steeply to Lost Creek and the headwaters
of the Oldman. Whitebark pine cling to its shale
slopes. To the west he steep wall of the Continental
Divide rises above alpine meadows.

The trail drops down into larch and fir forest,
wanders past an alpine tarn and crosses a steep
stream gully near the abandoned Galena Miracle
Mine. Mine timbers and the remainders of a cog
railway are strewn down a scree slope below the
mine shaft. A steep but rideable trail bypasses the
switchbacks of the mine road and crosses a meadow
to the seismic line near Memory Lake. From the lake,
7.1 km of good dirt road leads to the parking area at
the end of the Oldman River Road.

Jeff Gruttz ridge riding on the Great Divide Trail.
Cataract Plateau and Mount Farquhar in the background.

90 MAPS 37,38,40
LOW DIVIDE TRAIL

It is possible to ride from Cat Creek to the Oldman River entirely on backcountry roads. Jeff Grutz thought of the route and nicknamed it the Low Divide Trail in honour of its big brother to the west, the Great Divide Trail. The distance, 49.6 km, is not prohibitive, but it includes a lot of rough road for a one day ride. The maze of logging roads requires good navigational skills. No one has done the route in one day as of 1986, but some bicycle jock is bound to do it soon. Let me know if you do the trip.

DISTANCE
49.6 km
ELEVATION GAIN
1120 m (3700 ft)
MAPS
82 J/7 Mount Head
82 J/2 Fording River

NORTH ACCESS
Cat Creek picnic area on Kananaskis Trail (Hwy. 40), 5.6 km north of Highwood Junction.

SOUTH ACCESS
End of Oldman River Road, 28 km west of the Forestry Trunk Road (S.R. 940).

#	TRAIL NAME	MAP #	DISTANCE
76	Carnarvon Creek	37	5.6 km
78	Strawberry Hills	37	6.2 km
77	Fitzsimmons Creek	37	4.5 km
79	Baril Creek	37	0.4 km
81	Baril Loop	38	4.0 km
80	Etherington Creek	38	0.2 km
82	Raspberry Pass	38	6.1 km
88	Cataract Creek	38	1.2 km
88	Lost Creek	39	7.3 km
92	Oyster Creek	39	13.3 km
91	Headwaters of Oldman	39	1.0 km
	Total Distance		49.6 km

VARIATIONS
Rye Ridge trail from Etherington Creek to Cataract Creek (#80).
Great Divide Trail from Boy Scout bridge to Oldman River (#89).

Jo-Ann Draper exploring a dirt bike trail along Cabin Ridge. ⇨ High Rock Range and the the "Elevators" in the background.

OLDMAN

91 MAP 40
HEADWATERS OF
THE OLDMAN RIVER

This route follows a good dirt road up the Oldman River to Memory Lake near the Continental Divide. The Great Divide Trail can be hiked from the lake to an abandoned mine on the slopes of Mount Gass.

Cycle up a good dirt road past the beaver ponds and the meadows along the creek. At the 1 km point there is a rough road to the north. This is the start of the Oyster Creek - Lost Creek road which can be cycled 23 km north to Cataract Creek (#92). Ford Oyster Creek. Past the 2 km point, several hundred metres of the original road have been downgraded by the Forest Service to discourage vehicle access. Follow a steep trail to a seismic line which heads west to Memory Lake and the open slopes of Mount Gass. The mine roads can be seen from the lake.

The Great Divide Trail, which is marked by red paint blazes, crosses the seismic road 200 m east of the lake and leads north along the mine roads through larch forest and alpine meadows to the base of Mount Gass. If you look carefully, you can see mine timbers and the remains of a cog railway strewn down a scree slope below the shaft of the abandoned Galena Miracle Mine.

The seismic line offers a detour to Oyster Creek on the return trip.

RATING
Tough
DISTANCE
7.1 km to Memory Lake
TIME
3 hours return
ELEVATION GAIN
195 m (640 ft)
MAP
82 J/2 Fording River

ACCESS
From Highwood Junction, drive 48 km south on the Forestry Trunk Road (S.R. 940) to the Oldman River Road. Drive 28 km to the end of the Oldman River Road which ends at a beaver pond near Straight Creek.

Jo and the boys on the Oyster Creek road.
Jo-Ann Draper, Terry Merrit, Jeff Gruttz.

92 MAP 40
OYSTER EXCURSION
(OLDMAN RIVER
TO CATARACT CREEK)

The Oyster Excursion follows seismic and logging roads from the Oldman River to Cataract Creek. The route is used as a snowmobile route in the winter and it is marked with orange squares. Since it is a valley bottom route, it is far less attractive than the Great Divide Trail (#89), but at the same time requires less effort and is less time consuming.

From the end of the Oldman River Road cycle 1 km up a good dirt road and turn north on a seismic line that climbs up onto a grassy terrace. This good dirt road makes at least seven shallow crossings over Oyster Creek and there are some boggy areas to hike around. The valley bottom is a meadow of grasses and willow that turns golden brown in late summer. Beehive Mountain shows its distinct profile to the south.

The route over the low divide between Oyster and Lost Creeks follows a straight seismic line through spruce forest. Alberta Forest Service has scraped the road down to mineral soil in an effort to improve it as a snowmobile trail. Unfortunately, it did not improve its qualities as a cycling trail and it can be rather muddy when wet. The route eventually leaves the seismic line and follows a rough logging road that has been well trampled by elk and cattle.

It is a relief to reach the Boy Scout Bridge and a smooth gravel road which continues along Lost Creek and Cataract Creek (#88) for 13.2 km back to the Forestry Trunk Road.

RATING
Tough - dry weather only
DISTANCE
27.5 km one way
TIME
4 - 5 hours one way
ELEVATION GAIN
205 m (675 ft)
ELEVATION LOSS
345 m (1130 ft)
MAPS
82 J/2 Fording River
82 J/7 Mount Head

SOUTH ACCESS
From Highwood Junction, drive 48 km south along the Forestry Trunk Road (S.R. 940) to the Oldman River Road. Drive 28 km to the end of the Oldman River Road which ends at a beaver pond near Straight Creek.

NORTH ACCESS
From Highwood Junction, drive 11.6 km south on the Forestry Trunk Road (S.R. 940) to the Raspberry Fire Lookout access road. It lies 2 km north of Cataract Creek Recreation Area.

93 MAP 41
SHALE CREEK
TO CABIN RIDGE

This is a dirt bike trail that offers interesting cycling to excellent viewpoints on Cabin Ridge. The trip up is largely pushing but the trip back is a challenging downhill ride on a narrow trail. This south-facing route dries out early in the spring.

The trail starts in open, lodgepole pine forest. It drops sharply into a branch of Shale Creek then works its way up the valley through meadows. From the pass at the head of Shale Creek you can hike either north or south to gain the top of the ridge where you can see Tornado and Beehive mountains to the west, the Sugarloaf Fire Lookout to the south-west and the Livingstone Range to the east. Easy hiking along the ridge makes this a fascinating place to explore.

RATING
Terrific
DISTANCE
4.5 km one way
TIME
3 - 4 hours return
ELEVATION GAIN
490 m (1600 ft)
MAPS
82 G/16 Maycroft
82 J/1 Langford Creek

ACCESS
From the Forestry Trunk Road (S.R. 940), drive 8.2 km up the Oldman River Road. Look for a narrow unmarked trail on the east side of the road. It is 300 m north of the ford at the start of the Hidden Creek trail (#94).

Looking for easier cycling on Cabin Ridge. Sugarloaf Fire Lookout in the background.

MAP 41

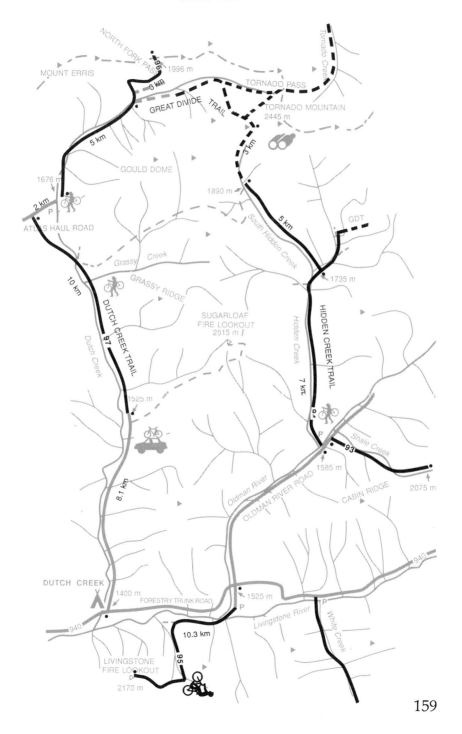

HIDDEN CREEK

Dirt roads lead up Hidden Creek and South Hidden Creek to the base of Tornado Mountain where the Great Divide Trail continues on to the North Notch of Tornado Mountain. Controversial logging operations have started in the South Hidden Creek Valley. A road has been built from the Dutch Creek road to the South Hidden Creek road and logs are being hauled south along the Atlas Haul Road to Coleman. The logging operations may change the South Hidden Creek road.

NORTH HIDDEN CREEK - The trip starts with a ford of the Oldman River which can be too deep to cross during high water in June and is knee deep and fast flowing in summer. Initially the four-wheel drive road parallels Hidden Creek which is out of sight from the road. En route, the Alberta Forest Service has dug several large tank traps to block four-wheel drive vehicles. The views of Tornado Mountain and Gould Dome keep getting better as you cycle up the road which provides some interesting up and down riding on smooth but rutted dirt. Just as your feet start to dry out the road swings south to cross Hidden Creek and a tributary in three successive crossings. Cycle 700 m further to the South Hidden Creek road which branches to the west (left).

SOUTH HIDDEN CREEK - The road climbs steadily but gently and varies from good dirt to boggy areas that will require some pushing. The road ends abruptly in the shadow of the peaks to the west.

RATING
Tough
DISTANCE
12 km one way
TIME
4 - 5 hours return
ELEVATION GAIN
305m (1000 ft)
MAPS
82 G/15 Tornado Mountain
82 G/16 Maycroft

ACCESS
The Oldman River Road branches off the Forestry Trunk Road (S.R. 940) 60.9 km south of Highwood Junction and 45.1 km north of Coleman. Drive 7.9 km west on the Oldman River Road to the confluence of the Oldman River and Hidden Creek. Look for an obvious ford on the west side of the Oldman River Road where the Hidden Creek road starts.

HIKING OPTION
NORTH TORNADO NOTCH
The Great Divide trail, marked with red paint blazes, can be picked up about 100 m from the end of the South Hidden Creek road. It offers a hike up steep, scree slopes to the spectacular notch immediately south of the main peak of Tornado Mountain. In 2.5 km it gains 555 m.

CYCLING OPTION
Because of the logging operations, a loop trip is now possible from Hidden Creek south to Dutch Creek and a return ride made along the Forestry Trunk Road and the Oldman River Road.

160

95 MAP 41
LIVINGSTONE FIRE LOOKOUT

The road to Livingstone Fire Lookout receives little use since the lookout is supplied by helicopter. It is one of the lower lookouts in the area and one of the few that are located below treeline.

The trail starts as a good gravel road. Take the right fork 0.5 km from the Forestry Trunk Road and cycle the rutted but smooth, dirt road to the Livingstone River. The road dips into the shale canyon to a ford that is 30 m wide and less than axle deep in midsummer. Continue south for 2 km to a large grassy meadow where the road becomes a faint rutted track. Watch for the obvious road to the east that disappears into the trees.

Intermittent pushing is required where the rocky road climbs up a canyon toward the crest of the Livingstone Range. Open slopes above the road are dotted with Douglas fir. The road improves to a finer shale surface as it climbs through spruce and fir forest. The summit ridge and peak provide good views of Tornado Mountain and Gould Dome to the west, while to the east Whaleback Ridge snakes through the foothills. Notice how the south faces of the gullies on Whaleback Ridge are grassland while the cooler north-facing slopes grow conifer trees.

The return ride is fast and enjoyable except for the rocky section in the canyon.

RATING
Terrific
DISTANCE
10.3 km
TIME
4 - 5 hours return
ELEVATION GAIN
705 m (2315 ft)
MAP
82 G/16 Maycroft

ACCESS
The trailhead lies on the east side of the Forestry Trunk Road (S.R. 940), 60.9 km south of Highwood Junction and 45.1 km north of Coleman. It is a gravel road directly opposite the Oldman River Road. Park near the Forestry Trunk Road since the lookout road is quite rough for driving and the bridge has been removed 2 km up the road.

96 MAP 41
NORTH FORK PASS

Upper Dutch Creek is a wild and remote valley teeming with wildlife and riddled with logging roads and cutblocks.

At the end of the Atlas Haul Road, ford Dutch Creek which is 15 m wide and axle deep in summer but much deeper during the peak flow in June. The road soon crosses Dutch Creek twice more although the crossings are much shallower. A good gravel road, better than mutch of the Atlas Haul Road, continues through mature spruce forest for 5 km to a distinct road branching to the east. Cycle up this road and cross Dutch Creek for the fourth time. Push up this dirt road to the top of the ridge which has been logged and has small pines regenerating among the slash. The huge mass of Gould Dome looms across the valley to the east. The road climbs gently into North Fork Pass and eventually reaches a rocky bluff giving a good view into British Columbia. It is possible to cycle down Line Creek and the Elk River road for 32 km to Sparwood.

When I last cycled this trail, I followed grizzly tracks all the way to North Fork Pass. Further up Dutch Creek, I saw two very large grizzly droppings on the road. At the same time I was assaulted by the smell of a well rotted carcass. Descriptions of how savagely grizzlies can defend animal carcasses flashed through my mind. My respect for grizzlies overcame my curiosity about the trail and I quickly laid another set of fat tire tracks down the valley.

RATING
Tender
DISTANCE
8 km one way
TIME
3 hours round trip
ELEVATION GAIN
320 m (1050 ft)
MAP
82 G/15 Tornado Mountain

ATLAS HAUL ROAD ACCESS
From Coleman, drive 5 km west on Highway 3 to the Allison Creek Road. Drive 2.5 km north to the fork at the cattle gate. The left fork goes past a fish hatchery to Chinook Lake campground. The right fork, known as the Atlas Haul Road, continues for 30.5 km past North and South Racehorse Creeks to a ford on Dutch Creek. It is not recommended in wet conditions when it gets rutted and slippery, or for small cars in any conditions.

DUTCH CREEK ACCESS
From the Forestry Trunk Road (S.R. 940) drive and cycle up the Dutch Creek road (#97) to the Atlas Haul Road. Cycle north on the Atlas Haul Road for 2 km to the trailhead.

HIKING / CYCLING OPTION
The GREAT DIVIDE TRAIL, a hiking trail marked with red paint blazes, continues up Dutch Creek Valley and over the steep North Notch of Tornado Mountain to the Hidden Creek road (#94).

97 MAP 41
DUTCH CREEK

The Dutch Creek road is a four-wheel drive road that is of little interest by itself but very useful as an access route to the North Fork trail.

The first 8.1 km of the road to the junction with the Sugarloaf Fire Lookout road, can be driven by most vehicles. Past the junction, the road gets too rutted and rough for driving although it is easy cycling on gravel and dirt through cutblocks and mature mixed forest. The massive Gould Dome rises to the north. The Dutch Creek road joins the Atlas Haul Road from Coleman. The Atlas Haul Road ends at a ford of Dutch Creek 2 km north of the junction. It is a further 8 km to North Fork Pass (#96).

In 1985, a logging road was built from the Dutch Creek road to Hidden Creek. This presents the possibility of a loop trip from Dutch Creek to Hidden Creek with a return ride on the Oldman River Road.

RATING
Tender
DISTANCE
12 km to North Fork Pass trailhead
TIME
2 - 3 hours return
ELEVATION GAIN
180 m (590 ft)
MAPS
82 G/15 Tornado Mountain
82 G/16 Maycroft

ACCESS
The Dutch Creek road starts from the north side of Dutch Creek campground on the Forestry Trunk Road (S.R. 940), 66.7 km south of Highwood Junction and 39.3 km north of Coleman.

Logging road leading to North Fork Pass. High Rock range in background.

163

MAP 42

MOUNT LIVINGSTONE

940

WESTRUP CREEK

CROWSNEST
FOREST BOUNDARY

1465 m

P

N

1735 m

Beaver Creek

99

10.5 km

1895 m

1.8 km

P

1.9 km

LIVINGSTONE
FALLS

1895 m

Riley Creek

1675 m

98

0.8 km

4.8 km

LIVINGSTONE RANGE

Ridge Creek

HORSESHOE
RIDGE

FORESTRY TRUNK ROAD

DEEP CREEK

1805 m

100

7 km

CHAFFEN RIDGE

Bruin Creek

940

Livingstone River

1.3 km

100

6.7 km

1675 m

BEAVER POND

White Creek

P

1525 m

98 MAP 42
BEAVER CREEK LOOP

This short loop trip on the lower slopes of Mount Livingstone makes a good bike ride from the Livingstone Falls campground. Apart from some rocky road on the south end of the loop, most of the trip is on smooth, gravel road.

After the dreary dirt road through the spruce stand at the trailhead, the road improves dramatically. It becomes a smooth, gravel road that rises gently through a cutblock. A splash of fireweed and the grey ghosts of spruce trees identify the site of a fire. At 1.8 km the road forks below a canyon at the south end of Mount Livingstone. The east fork climbs through the canyon and continues to Westrup Creek (#99). The south fork continues through the cutblock to a low pass giving a good view north to Plateau Mountain and west to the High Rock Range beyond the Oldman River.

Although Beaver Creek is shown on the maps flowing through the canyon south of Mount Livingstone, there is no water in the creek in summer. You might wonder how logging affects stream flow. Numerous studies around the world consistently show that removing the tree cover increases the stream flow from a watershed. The reason is that more water evaporates from a forest than from grassland, and since a forest has more surface area than grassland, greater transpiration of water takes place.

The smooth gravel road on the south side of the small pass gives a good downhill ride until it becomes rocky and rough where it enters the pine and poplar forest. Be sure to close any cattle gates and watch for raspberries and strawberries in late summer.

Return on the Forestry Trunk Road.

RATING
Tough
DISTANCE
9.3 km return
TIME
1 - 2 hours return
ELEVATION GAIN
220 m (720 ft)
MAP
82 J/1 Langford Creek

ACCESS
The trailhead is a rutted dirt road between mature spruce forest on the east side of the Forestry Trunk Road (S.R. 940), 1.9 km north of Livingstone Falls campground. The trailhead is 40.4 km south of Highwood Junction and 65.6 km north of Coleman.

165

99 MAP 42
BEAVER CREEK
TO WESTRUP CREEK

This trail, which takes you from logging country to ranching country, follows Beaver Creek over a low pass in the Livingstone Range to Westrup Creek on the east side. The Livingstone Range can be recrossed to make a return trip or a car shuttle can be arranged on the Chimney Rock Road. The drive from the west access to the east access is 65 km to the north via Johnson Creek Trail (S.R. 532) or 100 km to the south via Secondary Road 517.

Cycle up the Beaver Creek road for 1.8 km to the junction below the canyon at the south end of Mount Livingstone. Peddle and push up the rough, rocky canyon to a gate and beaver pond at the top of the canyon. A good, level dirt road continues through meadow and open forest and crosses the pass. The road soon drops on a smooth, shale surface down the east side of the Livingstone Range. Pass a dry grassy ridge with twisted weatherbeaten pines silhouetted against the skyline like a scene from a Japanese painting.

RATING
Terrific - dry weather only
DISTANCE
12.3 km one way
TIME
2 - 3 hours one way
ELEVATION GAIN
160 m (525 ft)
ELEVATION LOSS
430 m (1400 ft)
MAP
82 J/1 Langford Creek

WEST ACCESS
Via Beaver Creek Loop
(#98).

EAST ACCESS
From Chain Lakes Provincial Park drive 10.5 km south to Chimney Rock Road on the west side of Highway 22. Drive west for 3.5 km, take the right fork and continue for 7.7 km to the gate at the end of the gravel road.

166

Westrup Creek, showing the deep shale canyon where part of the road has collapsed. - photo Gillean Daffern

The deep Westrup Creek Valley never does give an open view to the east. From this point on, none of the roads marked on the topo maps are evident. The obvious route stays close to Westrup Creek, crossing it numerous times, all the way to the driveable gravel road. The upper creek follows a deep shale canyon where part of the road has collapsed and you must follow a narrow footpath. Further down the road, a large meadow covered in daisies gives a view of the steep eastern side of the Livingstone Range. The remaining rough dirt road is well travelled by cattle. Be sure to close the cattle gates.

CYCLING OPTION
Cyclists with a high energy level might consider combining this trip with route #101, using the Forestry Trunk Road (S.R.940) and the Chimney Rock Road as connectors. It is recommended you start from the White Creek end so as to take advantage of the steep drop down the eastern slope of the Livingstone Range.

100 MAP 42
WHITE CREEK

White Creek is a rough, dirt road that rises to the top of the Livingstone Range and provides an excellent view of Whaleback Ridge and Porcupine Hills. A beaver pond 8 km from the trailhead provides a destination for a shorter trip.

The trail starts by dropping into the canyon of the Livingstone River - the ford is about calf-deep and 15 m wide in July and August. A rutted, dirt road rises to a bench above the river and follows the edge of a deep canyon along the lower part of White Creek. After 2 km of riding through the forest, you emerge into a meadow and cross White Creek. Most of the rest of the trail follows meadows along the valley bottom. I counted 32 shallow creek crossings on the way to the top.

At 6.7 km, at a three-way fork in a meadow, the faint road to the south leads 1.3 km to a pleasant beaver pond. The pond is shallow but it is good enough for a skinny dip on a hot day.

The main road continues up the creek. At 7.8 km there is an outcrop of conglomerate rock embedded with igneous pebbles. The road is mostly rough and occasionally pitted by cattle hooves. The pine forest gives way to spruce - some of the hillsides grow Douglas fir. Be sure to close the cattle gates. At 13.7 km take the right fork and push up a steep hill to the top of the range. A short walk up the hill to the south will give you an excellent view of the sinuous Whaleback Ridge and the Porcupine Hills. Hawks can often be seen playing in the thermals along the ridge.

RATING
Tough - dry weather only
DISTANCE
13.7 km one way
TIME
5 - 7 hours return
ELEVATION GAIN
280 m (920 ft)
MAPS
82 G/16 Maycroft
82 J/1 Langford Creek

ACCESS
The trailhead is located on the east side of the Forestry Trunk Road (S.R. 940), 4 km north of the Oldman River Road, 56.9 km south of Highwood Junction and 49.1 km north of Coleman. A dirt road crosses a meadow for about 200 m to the Livingstone River.

CYCLING OPTION
It is possible to cycle the road down the steep eastern slope of the Livingstone Range to the Chimney Rock Road - a drop of 400 m in 5 km.

Crowsnest Mountain hovering over Chinook Lake. ⇨

CROWSNEST-CASTLE

101 MAP 43
DAISY CREEK –
VICARY SUMMIT LOOP

This long, easy loop trip follows Daisy Creek to its headwaters on Grassy Mountain and returns on the Forestry Trunk Road via Vicary Summit.

The DAISY CREEK ROAD starts as a rutted but smooth four-wheel drive road. It rolls up and down through the hills and later levels out in meadows along the creek. This is classic high foothill country with open pine and poplar forest and pleasant meadows. The Livingstone Range rises to the east. There are two wide shallow crossings of Daisy Creek. At 11.5 km take the right fork - the road here is a faint dirt track in a meadow. The right fork is a straight seismic line which leads over a thickly forested hill to the Coseka Resources road, a gas well access road.

The COSEKA RESOURCES ROAD offers fast easy cycling on a high-grade gravel road which passes a sour gas dehydration plant and several side roads leading to gas wells.

The road crosses the pass between Daisy Creek and Blairmore Creek, a wide rolling ridge on the north side of Grassy Mountain. You are in for a good ride as the smooth gravel road drops in huge switchbacks down the west side of the mountain. Where the Coseka Resources road joins the Forestry Trunk Road there is a good view back to Grassy Mountain with its maze of coal mining roads and to The Chief which can be seen to the south.

The 22.1 km return trip on the Forestry Trunk Road is a fast, easy cycle on a wide gravel road. After Vicary Summit it is downhill almost all the way to Daisy Creek.

RATING
Tender
DISTANCE
44.6 km round trip
TIME
4 - 6 hours
ELEVATION GAIN
540 m (1775 ft)
MAPS
82 G/16 Maycroft
82 G/9 Blairmore

NORTH ACCESS
Daisy Creek crosses the Forestry Trunk Road (S.R. 940) 75 km south of Highwood Junction and 31 km north of Coleman. The trailhead is the four-wheel drive road 170 m north of the Daisy Creek bridge.

SOUTH ACCESS
The Coseka Resources road is a good gravel road that joins the Forestry Trunk Road 7.8 km north of Coleman. It is marked by a distinctive sign made with a section of "big inch" steel pipe.

102 MAP 43
GRASSY MOUNTAIN TO DAISY CREEK

The Blairmore Creek road continues north past
Grassy Mountain to Daisy Creek. It makes a 44.3 km
loop trip possible with the Coseka Resources road
and the Forestry Trunk Road. If you are more ambitious, a 66.9 km loop can be made by continuing
down Daisy Creek to the Forestry Trunk Road.

The Blairmore Creek road continues north past the
four-way junction south of Grassy Mountain as a
smooth, dirt road. The road forks 3 km from the
junction. The left fork ends in the open pit mines on
Grassy Mountain while the right fork drops down to
Gold Creek and continues north. The road gets
rougher as it climbs over the low pass to Daisy Creek.
At Daisy Creek take the left fork which is a seismic
line following the creek. It is a faint track through a
meadow where it joins the other seismic line going
south to the Coseka Resources road.

RATING
Tough
DISTANCE
11 km
TIME
2 - 3 hours one way
ELEVATION GAIN
280 m (920 ft)
ELEVATION LOSS
160 m (525 ft)
MAPS
82 G/9 Blairmore
82 G/16 Maycroft

SOUTH ACCESS
Via Blairmore Creek road
(#103).

NORTH ACCESS
Via Daisy Creek road (#101).

MAP 43

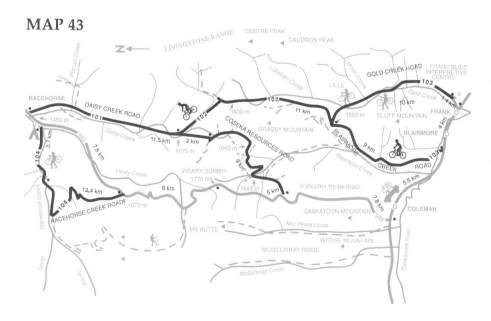

171

103 MAP 43
GRASSY MOUNTAIN – GOLD CREEK LOOP

This loop trip is good cycling in dry weather. The roughest cycling occurs on the lower part of the Gold Creek road, a slightly rutted dirt road that can be muddy in the spring. The fords are shallow in summer but could be a problem during runoff. The Blairmore Creek road is a smooth all-weather road built on the old railway bed and surfaced with black tailings from the abandoned coal mine on Grassy Mountain. The trail passes several modern and historic features of energy resource exploitation.

The GOLD CREEK road can be confusing as it passes a natural gas pipeline and branches several times. Stay with the most obvious road closest to the creek. After riding through a tunnel of poplar trees and crossing several fords, the trail enters a large meadow which is the abandoned townsite of Lille. The Lille area is designated as a provincial historic site by Alberta Culture and it is illegal to disturb it. The road past Lille uses the bed of the former railway from Lille to the coal mines.

The town of Lille experienced a boom and bust cycle common to many Canadian one company resource towns. Coal was discovered there in 1901. West Canadian Collieries was organized with foreign capital (French) and a railway was built. Lille grew rapidly to a town of more than 300 people supported by the mine. By 1913 there was little demand for coke so the mine closed and the fledging town perished. Nothing is left but a few foundations and coke ovens. A 500 kilovolt powerline, built in 1984, crosses the road north of Lille. It runs from Cranbrook, through Phillips Pass and north to Langdon, near Calgary, allowing power to flow both ways between Alberta and B.C.

Further on, open seams of coal and many excavations can be seen on Grassy Mountain. The open pit mining on Grassy Mountain took place about forty years after the demise of the town of Lille.

RATING
Tender
DISTANCE
24.4 km round trip
TIME
4 - 6 hours return
ELEVATION GAIN
275 m (900 ft)
MAP
82 G/9 Blairmore

ACCESS
Between the town of Frank and the Frank Slide, on the east side of Gold Creek, follow the paved access road for the Frank Slide Interpretive Centre. Drive north on this road for about 1 km. Take the left fork onto the gravel road. At the 1.4 km point, park at a four-wheel drive dirt road that forks to the left. Please respect the fact that much of the route passes through private property.

BLAIRMORE ACCESS
If you choose to ride up the Blairmore Creek road, the start of the road can be found on the north side of Highway 3 at the main access to Blairmore (24th Avenue and 129th Street). It is a gravel road that leads north through the abandoned Greenhill Mine.

BLAIRMORE CREEK ROAD - From the four-way junction, the road to the west climbs to the mine site on Grassy Mountain. The Blairmore Creek road continues north for 10 km to Daisy Creek (#102) and can be cycled all the way down Daisy Creek to the Forestry Trunk Road (S.R. 940).

The return ride to Blairmore is a fast smooth ride offering a good view west to Crowsnest Mountain. Although the Blairmore Creek road is driveable and open to traffic, few vehicles venture onto it. En route, watch for artifacts from a former railway including a coal tipple, rusted signs, abandoned wooden coal cars and part of the original railway grade.

The road later passes through the Greenhill Mine, a provincial historic site on the north side of Blairmore. There are many old buildings including a power plant and a shed full of core samples.

It is a 4 km cycle back to Frank along Highway 3.

Jo-Ann Draper riding through the townsite of Lille.
Open pit coal mines on Grassy Mountain.

104 MAP 43
RACEHORSE CREEK LOOP

The Racehorse Creek road heads upstream from Racehorse Creek campground and eventually returns to the Forestry Trunk Road further south. Most of the loop is on driveable road.

Start the trip by fording Vicary Creek near the campground past the cattle gate. A smooth but rutted four-wheel drive road follows the creek through open pine and poplar forest and meadows. There are three fords of Racehorse Creek - the first occuring by a small sandstone canyon. After the last ford, the road improves to a high grade gravel road. This section is a favourite camping spot of local people who know about this secluded and unmarked road. The road climbs up switchbacks south of the creek and follows the contours back to the Forestry Trunk Road.

RATING
Tender
DISTANCE
23.9 km round trip
TIME
2 - 4 hours return
ELEVATION GAIN
225 m (740 ft)
MAPS
82 G/16 Maycroft
82 G/15 Tornado Mountain

ACCESS
Park at Racehorse Creek campground on the west side of the Forestry Trunk Road (S.R. 940), 76.3 km south of Highwood Junction and 29.7 km north of Coleman. The trailhead lies at the west side of the campground at a cattle gate where the Racehorse Creek road crosses Vicary Creek.

CYCLING OPTION
VICARY CREEK MINE ROAD - I have never explored the area, but a road loops to the west and crosses a high pass where there are several abandoned mines. There could be some interesting cycling there.

Ford on Racehorse Creek near the Forestry Trunk Road.

105 MAP 44
DEADMAN PASS –
PHILLIPPS PASS LOOP

This long loop trip crosses two low passes on the Continental Divide. Except for a 2.5 km-long ski trail at the beginning, the entire trip is on road surrounded by open pine forest. There are many variations to this trip because of the many road access points.

DEADMAN PASS - Chinook Lake is a pretty little foothills lake dwarfed by the isolated mass of Crowsnest Mountain. From the ski trail sign at the boat ramp, a wide trail follows the shore of the lake. It deteriorates to a bumpy narrow trail in a wet valley bottom before joining the smooth four wheel drive road from the Atlas snowmobile area. The decaying remains of a logging camp can be found near the small pond at the junction. A root cellar, or possibly a dynamite cache, is dug into the bank at the side of the road.

The road rises gently through open pine and poplar forest to Deadman Pass. Numerous seismic lines branch off to both sides. There is an oddity in the Alberta - British Columbia boundary marked on the map. The boundary supposedly coincides with the Divide, and yet a stream flows from the Alberta side to the B.C. side.

At Deadman Pass take the fork to the left which plunges into a tunnel of alders and is occasionally flooded by beavers. The road returns to dry pine forest and a view opens up to Erickson Ridge.

The ALEXANDER CREEK ROAD is a smooth but rutted, dirt, four-wheel drive road. It follows the contours as the river drops away into the valley, eventually descending to Highway 3.

PHILLIPPS PASS - Cycle 1 km west on the pavement to Crowsnest Provincial Park. At the north end of the park, an obvious gravel pipeline road climbs up toward Phillipps Pass which is open and invariably windy. The wind howls through the power lines and the gondola that provides technicians with access to the microwave tower on Crowsnest Ridge. Phillipps Lake is a sink lake at the top of the pass. This is your chance to go swimming across the Continental Divide.

RATING
Tough
DISTANCE
38 km round trip
TIME
5 - 8 hours round trip
ELEVATION GAIN
525 m (1700 ft)
MAP
82 G/10 Crowsnest

ACCESS
The Allison Creek Road is 5 km west of Coleman on the Crowsnest Highway (Hwy. 3). Drive north 2.5 km, take the left fork and continue another 3.5 km to Chinook Lake campground. The trailhead is at the ski trail sign at the boat ramp.

ALTERNATE ACCESS
#1/ Drive up the Allison Creek Road and the Atlas Haul Road 6.5 km to the Atlas snowmobile area. Cycle the four-wheel drive road to the west for 1.5 km to where it merges with the ski trail from Chinook Lake.
#2/ The east end of the Phillipps Pass road joins a residential road at the east end of Crowsnest Lake, 9 km west of Coleman.
#3/ The west end of Phillipps Pass road starts from Crowsnest Provincial Park 2 km west of Crowsnest Pass. From the north end of the park, an obvious pipeline road leads uphill to the pass.

The gravel road on the east side of the pass drops steeply down to meadows alongside Crowsnest Lake.

It is a 10 km cycle on Highway 3 and the Allison Creek Road back to Chinook Lake.

CYCLING OPTION
For a more ambitious adventure tour, you might consider making a loop trip north along Alexander Creek, crossing either Racehorse or North Fork Pass (#96) and returning on the Atlas Haul Road.

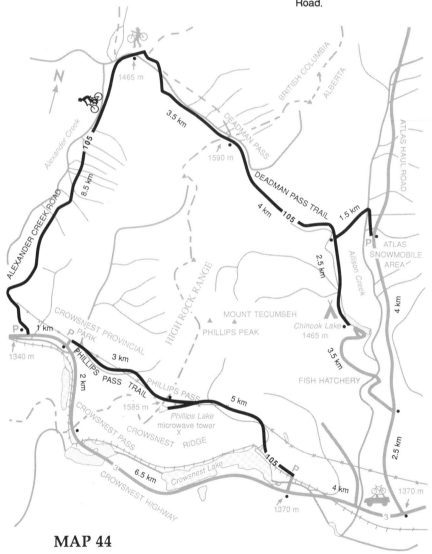

MAP 44

176

106 MAP 45
CASTLE RIVER

From the tank trap at Scarpe Creek, this cycling route follows a logging road up the Castle River to the Castle River Divide which separates the Castle drainage from Bauerman Creek (#110) in Waterton Lakes National Park. The upper Castle River is a beautiful and remote valley with a good to smooth, dirt and gravel road. Numerous culverts have been removed, leaving deep dips at the streams that can be challenging to ride through.

The road forks 1 km from the trailhead. The left fork, which immediately climbs a short steep hill, offers a rough ride where the road has been "put to bed". The right fork is a smooth road but there are four knee-deep fords of the fast flowing Castle River which can be difficult to cross in early summer. Both roads join after 1.4 km so take your choice of difficulties. At 4.6 km the Font Creek road branches to the south and crosses the river.

Past Font Creek the distinctive red shale slopes of Avion Ridge come into view and the subalpine valley becomes more open as you cycle through the more recent cutblocks. The last ford, east of Sage Mountain is about 4 m wide and less than axle deep. The rideable road ends in a spruce and fir forest at the base of a 500 m vertical wall of limestone.

RATING
Tough
DISTANCE
12.0 km one way to end of road
TIME
3 - 5 hours round trip
ELEVATION GAIN
210 m (700 ft)
MAP
82 G/1 Sage Creek

ACCESS
From the hamlet of Beaver Mines drive south-west for 14.1 km on Secondary Road 774 to the turnoff to Beaver Mines Lake. Follow this road south-east for 4 km to the gravel road which leads south up the Castle River. This rough road can be driven for 18.3 km to the tank trap which blocks the road at Scarpe Creek.

HIKING OPTIONS
CASTLE RIVER DIVIDE AND AVION RIDGE HIKE - A trail to the south climbs 275 m in 1.2 km to the Castle River Divide. Unfortunately, the pass is in the trees and there is no view. A trail to the east climbs up onto Avion Ridge which offers spectacular views in all directions.

Jo-Ann Draper and Colynn Kerr on the Castle River road. Avion Ridge in the background.

107 MAP 45
FONT CREEK

The Font Creek trail follows the logging road along Font Creek between Mount Matkin and Sage Mountain. It is a less attractive cycling route than the Castle River but can be made more interesting if combined with a hike to the col overlooking the headwaters of the Castle River.

The junction of the Font Creek road and the Castle River road is reasonably obvious. The remains of a bridge over the Castle River lie on the banks so you will have to ford the river which is about 20 m wide and thigh deep. Grind your gears up the rough, moderately steep, dirt road on the east bank of Font Creek. Avoid the steeper and rougher roads that branch to the left. After two shallow fords, the road climbs to the base of a high limestone face along the Continental Divide and eventually deteriorates to the point where you'll find walking preferable to cycling. It is just a short hike along the creek through subalpine forest to the col on the south end of Sage Mountain that overlooks the Castle Valley.

RATING
Tough - dry weather only
DISTANCE
4.0 km one way
TIME
2 hours round trip
ELEVATION GAIN
215 m (700 ft)
MAP
82 G/1 Sage Creek

ACCESS
Via Castle River trail (#106) at the 4.6 km point.

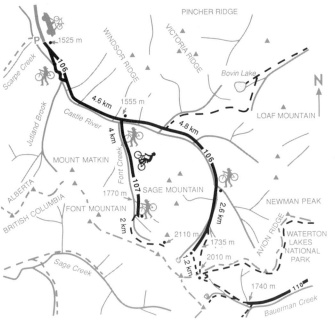

MAP 45

Jo-Ann Draper on Park Line trail in Waterton National Park. ⇨
"Where the prairie meets the mountains."

WATERTON PARK

108 MAP 46
KISHINENA CREEK VIA AKAMINA PASS

The Akamina Pass trail in Waterton Park is a designated bicycle trail providing access to the logging and exploration roads along Akamina Creek and Kishinena Creek. It makes a great one-way trip with a car shuttle if you can talk someone into dropping you off in Waterton, driving over Logan Pass and picking you up at the Flathead River. People used to drive this cycling route before the Tank Trap was built. East of Kishinena Bridge, Kishinena Road is still good enough to drive your new Toyota on.

Grind your gears up the wide, smooth trail to Akamina Pass. The sign at the summit says it is 22 miles (35 km) to Flathead but it is actually over 70 km.

RATING
Tough
DISTANCE
52.4 km to Flathead Bridge
TIME
6 - 9 hours one way
ELEVATION GAIN
315 m (1040 ft)
ELEVATION LOSS
690 m (2260 ft)
MAPS
82 G/1 Sage Creek
82 G/2 Inverted Ridge

EAST ACCESS
From Waterton Park townsite follow the Akamina Highway toward Cameron Lake for 13 km to the signed trailhead pull-off for Akamina Pass. The wide trail, blocked by boulders, lies on the west side of the road.

MAP 46

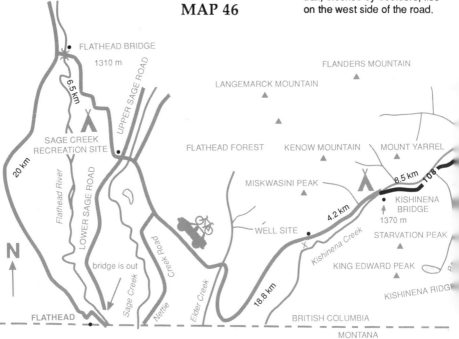

The road is narrow and smooth and you are forced to stop often to lift your bike over fallen trees. Dense spruce and fir forest blocks the view. The Tank Trap, where the road has been trenched for over 300 m by a backhoe to block off-road vehicles, starts 5.5 km past Akamina Pass. Past the Tank Trap the road passes in and out of cutblocks and gradually improves to become a high grade gravel road by the time the well site at Miskwasini Peak is reached. The wide, deep Kishinena Valley is surrounded by the peaks of the Border Ranges. There is a movement to declare this corner of British Columbia a Provincial Park.

North of Grizzly Gulch a game trail crosses the road to a rusted iron pipe, the remains of an early exploration well near the creek. Water seeps out of the pipe, carrying minerals to the surface and forming a salt lick for deer and elk. What appears to be the wooden drum for the winch gathers moss among the trees.

WEST ACCESS

The car shuttle from Waterton Park to Flathead Bridge is a 250 km drive. Follow highways 6, 17 and 89 to Saint Mary, Montana. Drive the "Going to the Sun Road" over Logan Pass to Apgar, then find the road which follows the Flathead River past Polebridge to the Flathead Customs station on the Canada - U.S. border. It is only open from 9 AM to 5 PM. Continue north about 20 km to the Kishinena Road and the bridge over the Flathead River. The Kishinena Road is a high grade gravel road suitable for travel by a small car as far as Kishinena Bridge. With a truck, the road could be driven as far as the bridge on Akamina Creek.

ALTERNATE WEST ACCESS

If you are heading north from Flathead Bridge, follow the Flathead Road, Harvey Creek Road, Lodgepole Road and Morrissey Road to Morrissey on Highway 3, 13 km south of Fernie. The route sounds complicated but it is one continuous gravel road. Kilometre signs count down from 74 at Flathead Bridge to 0 at Morrissey.

NOTE

The bridge over the Flathead River at the Flathead Customs Station has been taken out even though it is still shown on some maps. The river is too deep to ford, therefore the Sage Creek Road cannot be used as an access to the Kishinena Road.

181

Cross the bridge at the four-way junction. The 114 km sign is the start of a series of signs that count down to 74 km at Flathead Bridge and 0 km at Morrissey. Near Beavertail Creek, a long exciting hill surrounded by avalanche chutes provides a good downhill ride. At Kishinena Bridge there is a sandstone canyon and a pleasant primitive campsite. The road improves to a high grade gravel road at the well site. Shell drilled a wildcat well here in 1986 in a search for carbon dioxide which is used for enhanced recovery in oil wells. The smooth, gravel road to Flathead Bridge rolls up and down across the drainages of Elder Creek, Nettie Creek and Sage Creek through several large stands of western larch.

If you make it to Flathead Customs Station, be sure to talk to Border Bob and Ranger Rick. Maybe they remember the lady who left her purse there while trying to cross the border after closing time in search of two stray mountain bikers.

Colynn Kerr riding down a long screaming hill near Beavertail Creek on the Kishinena Road.

182

109 MAP 47
PARK LINE TRAIL

The Park Line trail was built to assist in patrolling the north-east corner of Waterton Park. This becomes especially important in hunting season when hunters find that elk and deer have an annoying habit of heading for the nearest game preserve when they are disturbed.

The trail, a rough and rutted road that is mostly vegetated, is not recommended in wet weather when the wheel ruts collect water. There is a shallow ford on Galwey Creek. As you climb the shoulder of Lakeview Ridge, there is a good view back toward the Lewis Range. The rest of the trip is characteristic of the lower foothills ranching country with its forest of stunted trembling aspens. The trail ends at the Oil Basin Warden Cabin, a name is indicative of the gas exploration and extraction north of Waterton Park.

RATING
Tough - dry weather only
DISTANCE
6.5 km one way
TIME
2 - 4 hours round trip
ELEVATION GAIN
280 m (920 ft)
MAP
82 H/4 Waterton Lakes

ACCESS
Drive to the Buffalo Paddock 2.2 km north of the park gate on Highway 6. Drive 1.5 km west to the end of the Buffalo Paddock road.

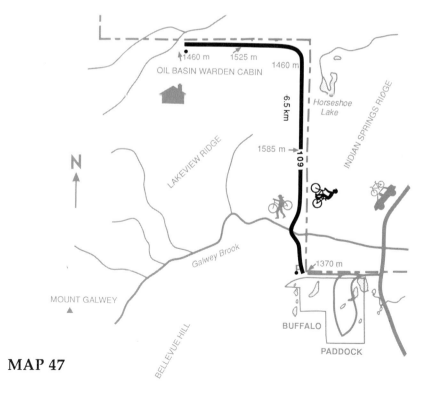

MAP 47

183

110 MAP 48
SNOWSHOE TRAIL

This former access road to the Snowshoe Warden Cabin provides good cycling on a gravel road. Its main attraction is the access it provides to several very good hiking trails which can now be hiked in a day trip.

The road follows the north side of Bauerman Creek. Anderson Peak rises to the south and the red shale on the lower slopes of Avion Ridge can be seen to the north. Where the bridges have been removed, there are several shallow stream crossings to negotiate. Cycling is allowed only as far as Snowshoe Cabin. The backcountry campsite provided near the cabin is in a not very scenic location.

RATING
Tender
DISTANCE
8.2 km one way to Snowshoe Cabin
TIME
2 - 3 hours return
ELEVATION GAIN
245 m (800 ft)
MAP
82 G/1 Sage Creek

ACCESS
From the Waterton townsite road (Hwy. 5), drive up the Red Rock Canyon Road to its terminus at Red Rock Canyon. The trail starts at the bridge on the west side of the parking lot.

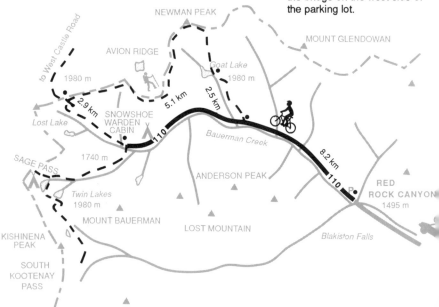

MAP 48

Jo-Ann Draper on the Snowshoe Trail in Waterton National Park.

HIKING OPTIONS

GOAT LAKE
Four kilometres from Red Rock Canyon the Goat Lake trail branches to the north. It is a steep 2.5 km hike to alpine meadows around the lake. Mountain goats are often seen on the rock wall above the lake.

AVION RIDGE
From Snowshoe Cabin, hike the Castle Divide trail to the top of the pass from where it's an 8 km hike along the ridge back to Goat Lake. This is a demanding skyline hike with spectacular views.

LOST LAKE
This is the shortest hike from Snowshoe Cabin (1.8 km). Follow the Castle River Divide trail for about 1 km to the Lost Lake trail. This is a beautiful valley with many signs of avalanche activity.

TWIN LAKES
BLUE GROUSE BASIN
SAGE PASS
SOUTH KOOTENAY PASS
From Snowshoe Cabin it is a 3.1 km hike to Twin Lakes. Several hikes can be made in this beautiful alpine area.

INDEX